SURVIVING THE MIDDLE MILES

26.2 Ways To Cross the Finish Line
With Your Customers

Darryl Rosen

authorHOUSE®

AuthorHouse™
1663 Liberty Drive, Suite 200
Bloomington, IN 47403
www.authorhouse.com
Phone: 1-800-839-8640

First published by AuthorHouse 11/6/2007

ISBN: 978-1-4343-4927-9 (sc)
ISBN: 978-1-4343-4926-2 (hc)

Printed in the United States of America
Bloomington, Indiana
This book is printed on acid-free paper.

Welcome to the start of what is sure to be a successful journey!

Surviving the Middle Miles is simple, but not easy. It's simple to want a business loved by customers and associates alike; but it's not easy to do everything it takes to achieve that goal. This book will help! In it, there are 26.2 chapters (or miles), each with many ideas, thoughts and suggestions designed to help you reap the rewards of crossing the finish line with your customers.

Should you read this book? You bet! Do you actively build and maintain relationships with both customers and clients? Are you a leader or manager with the responsibility of motivating your associates to provide exceptional customer service? Do you rely on customers and clients to help you pay the bills?

If you answered yes to any of the questions above, then you will benefit from this book.

I'm delighted to share my lessons from a lifetime of wine and spirit retailing. Can you apply these tips and suggestions to your line of work? Absolutely! Delighting customers and associates is all about relationships, and that's the truth no matter what business you're in!

After you've crossed the finish line, I would love to hear from you with your feedback and comments.

Thank you!
Darryl Rosen

P.S. Please visit www.survivingthemiddlemiles.com for more information.

This book is dedicated to my wife, Jill Rosen.

Jill, we walked down the aisle to the song *"Endless love"*, and you've given me that since the day I met you.

I love crossing the finish line with you there waiting!

CONTENTS

THE START

Win success in business by surviving the middle miles.

I started running marathons when I was 13 years old, the same year I began working in the family business. In those days, I thought the practices of running and working were simple and easy, I didn't know any better. After college, and a couple years of public accounting, I got a big shot of reality.

In the early 90's, our family business, Sam's Wines & Spirits, a Chicagoland institution started by my grandfather in the 1940's, experienced exponential growth. Despite the fact that it took 40+ years to occur, it seemed to happen overnight. We weren't operating a *shop* anymore, but a real business. We experienced many typical growing pains, and I realized that the only *simple* part was the simplicity of my thinking.

Around that time I ratcheted up my marathon running, and I tried to qualify for the *Boston Marathon.* 26.2 miles! Today, 26.2 feet would pose a challenge but back then, things were different. For those of you with any semblance of sanity who have resisted the lunacy of the marathon distance, *Boston* represents the Mecca for marathon runners. It is hallowed ground, and they don't just let anybody run. You have to run a qualifying time in another marathon before you gain entry into *Boston,* the oldest marathon in the United States.

I thought it would be simple and easy. That was my first mistake! How hard could it be? I mean, I ran in high school. Picture me with long locks (translation: not bald), hair blowing in the wind. Coeds sighing as I run by. Ok, not that last part! But running seemed much easier than a sport like football, with its requisite zones and blitzes, offenses and defenses.

I trained that entire summer. I was fast, fit, strong and ready; and more than a little full of myself. Listen to the experts and run a conservative pace? Not a chance! I toed the line that October morning. "Just do it!" I told myself as I laced my shoes. The gun went off and for reasons still unclear to me many years later; I took off like I was running the 100-yard dash! Just like that little road runner from the Saturday morning cartoons. By 10 miles I was struggling, by 12 miles I was walking and by 14 miles *I was looking for a taxi!* I was done.

I was unable to *survive the middle miles;* the part of the race where the excitement of the start has faded and you can't yet imagine the taste of the finish line. As a result, I never crossed the finish line that unseasonably warm Sunday morning.

In the middle miles the real race begins.

We experienced a similar phenomenon in our business. In the early years, customers were always cheering, much like people do at the start of a race. It seemed like everybody loved us. We were new and exciting. As we grew, we ran right into the middle miles trap; only we didn't know it at the time. Conditions were changing all around us. Competition was fierce. We were caught between stages, transforming from shopkeepers to real business people. We looked for ways to differentiate ourselves, to stand out from the growing crowd of competitors around us. What seemed simple was far from easy.

How did we do it? What was our secret? How did we build a business that won major industry awards such as the Market Watch Retailer of the Year and the Wine Enthusiast Retailer of the Year, not to mention the hearts and wallets of several hundred thousand happy customers each year? We stayed on course with our customers. We concentrated on what was important to our customers. We served our customers like no other wine and spirit retailer and developed an unrivaled reputation around the world.

We made the little things count. We hired the best people, then aggressively trained, motivated and retained them. We traveled around the world to source the best wines. What else did we do? Keep reading this book, and you'll learn some of the secrets of our success.

We survived the middle miles.

Will you ever have to *survive the middle miles*? Of course! Anything worth having, doing or accomplishing forces you to spend some time in the middle miles. Have you ever set a goal and had to work hard to achieve that goal? Then you know the feeling. Maybe it's wooing a new customer or spearheading your company's new customer service initiative. Have you ever opened a new business, started a new job, or worked on an important project? To be successful with such endeavors, you have to get through the lean times. Perhaps, you're pursuing a goal such as running a marathon or losing a few pounds. It doesn't matter because it's all the same. The middle miles await you.

In the beginning, everybody is cheering. It's exciting. It's new. It's fun. As you work your way forward in time, the fun slowly dissipates. Interest and encouragement from the early supporters begins to wane. The problem in the middle miles is that it's too early to see the results that will occur with perseverance and patience. Many get disillusioned. Many get lonely, frustrated and aggravated. Some stop trying. Others quit, like I did in the 1989 Chicago Marathon.

This book gives you 26.2 ways to cross the finish line with your customers. When you complete a marathon you get a medal, sore legs for a week, and a great feeling of accomplishment.

In business, the stakes are much higher. When customers cross your finish line, the awards ceremony features repeat and referral business, loyal customers and brand advocates. If you really execute well, then your customers will sing your praises for all to hear. You will hire and retain the best associates and they will be motivated to consistently deliver the best service. The best news may be that customers and clients will resist pressure to switch to your competitors. The end result will be a happy, healthy, profitable business.

Congratulations! By reading this book you obviously have the courage to start the race. I'll see you in the finisher's tent!

IF YOU LEAD, EMULATE WINNERS

People who succeed look to winners for inspiration.

Douglas McArthur once said that "Old soldiers never die; they just fade away." But the general never met my dad, who this week begins his own process of fading away after serving on the front lines of wine and spirits retailing for three generations. Recently, my family gave up control of the business we operated for many years. I started writing and speaking and he stayed to help the business he built. After a while, he and the business parted ways.

Was it the right time? We'll probably never know; but just last week, I spoke at a luncheon that he attended as my guest. Despite the fact that his days with the company were numbered, he was a consummate professional. He continued promoting the business; making sure to tell everyone at our table about the fantastic new store the company was planning. He had way too much passion and energy to leave so soon, but so it goes.

Ask anybody that ever called on him. He treated people with the utmost respect. He never belittled a salesperson, either privately or publically. He knew that salespeople had to put children through college, just like he did. If you needed a favor, you called my dad and considered it done. His word was good as gold. As the business changed, he gracefully moved over and allowed others do things he had always done. He was charitable and generous. Over the years, he helped hundreds of different charities with their special events. One thing was

5

always constant; nothing stopped him from his usual morning ritual of *getting the trucks out*, not even the blizzard of 1967.

To be sure, my dad was far from perfect. He was old school. He had a very strange *sense of fashion*. He sometimes crossed the line of being the employer; instead, preferring the role of a caring "father figure" type to all the lives he touched. Sometimes, he raised his voice. Sometimes he complained. We sparred from time to time, like any father and son. His crime was caring too much about the business. He devoted his life to the business and right or wrong in his style, he deserves so much credit for his contributions.

He passed many virtues to me. I didn't always know it at the time, but his lessons were helping me to be successful both in business and in my personal life. In tribute to his 50-plus years of service, I'd like to share some of his most successful character traits. Did he go about everything the right way? Of course not! Does anybody? He did, however, *cross the finish line* with thousands and thousands of customers and associates over the last 50 years. He must have been doing something right!

Here are some reasons why he ran such a successful business.

- **Tenacity** – he never gave up.

Author H.G. Wells once said, "The path of least resistance is the path of the loser." Fred never took the easy way. He had tenacity like I've never seen before or since. The same nature that made him a success on the basketball court 50 years ago (and still today on some courts!) made him a success in business. When the phone rang, he thought everybody should jump at it. To him, it was an honor that customers would call us. He never relied on anybody else to do the work for him. He didn't feel that it was up to anyone else to make him give his best. He just did it. No task was *beneath* him! His goal was simple -- to run the most successful wine and spirit business in town. He strived for this every day of his professional life.

Crossing the finish line with customers and associates requires great tenacity, persistence and stubbornness. Great customer service companies are persistent. They never stop delivering great service. They never stop talking about customers. They never stop trying to improve relationships with their customers. They make the little things count. They consistently reward and value their associates. They visualize reaching the finish line and doggedly pursue the goal of repeat and referral business.

- **Treating others with dignity** – he made friends, not enemies.

In 25 years of working with my dad, I can't remember one person who left the company because of him, but I can remember many who left because of others. Our competitors had a healthy respect for him. He never made fun of or mocked people.

Often, a local salesperson would pay a visit with his or her National Sales Manager in tow. To be sure, it was an extremely important day for the local account representative. Dad was certain to make him or her look like a hero, always sure to point out at least one great thing the salesperson was doing to sell more products in our stores. He was a natural at making you feel like the most important people in the world to him at that moment. If he was helping a customer within earshot of a salesperson, then he always recommended and tried to sell the product represented by that salesperson. He never kept people waiting. He did all he could to make customers look good. He yelled from time to time, (something I am against 100% in the workplace), but he never did it maliciously.

Treat everybody with whom you come in contact with great dignity. Never make people feel small. Don't gossip behind people's backs. Don't keep people waiting, a tactic some use as a display of power. If you have to give feedback, then do so in a professional manner. Have fun with others, but not at their expense. Always remember that what goes around, comes around.

You never know what the future holds. Today somebody may represent the 20th biggest brand in the market and the inclination may be to push them off because they're not a big fish. Don't do it! One day in the future, they may represent the 4th biggest brand, and one that is far more important to your business than you could ever imagine. You'll be glad you treated them with dignity.

- **Follow through** – he did what he said he would do!

When my dad said he was going to do something, he did it. When he said he would buy 500 cases of Chateau so–and–so, he followed through; sometimes, to my chagrin. I always favored a little less inventory. He followed through with customers and hated it when our associates failed to do the same. He always called customers back right away. He never procrastinated. (Maybe I got that wonderful trait from my mother!) He made customers feel important. The result: distributors and suppliers awarded us plenty of business because he always kept his word with them. He was their "go to" guy.

It's vital to always keep our word with customers and associates. If we say we're going to do something, we must do it. Many businesses fall short on this. At dinner one evening, I ordered a pasta dish that was prepared with the wrong sauce. The owner of the restaurant happened to come by. He asked me to try the dish and he would have it re-made if I wanted. He never came back to the table. Needless to say, his failure to follow through left a bad taste in my mouth.

Return emails and phone calls promptly. Keep your customers and associates informed. When you encounter problems, tell them. Be straight forward and honest. Customers aren't as unhappy when things go wrong as long as you're up front with them. Communicate the bad news, just as readily as you would convey good news. It's simple, but not easy. Simple to say you will call somebody back, but not easy to find the time or inclination to follow through with people consistently. As the Nike ads say, *"Just do it!"*

- **Be a part of the community** – he had a soft heart.

I'd call it generous to a fault. He loaned money to everyone, including members of the local community. When we cut back on employee loans (as a company), he still helped people out of his own pocket. For years, our main store was in an economically depressed neighborhood. He helped everybody. He had a kind word for the people who crossed his path. *He never considered himself better than anybody.* The *down on their luck* members of the neighborhood called him "Freddy", and me, "little Freddy." It was an honor! He may have accomplished more than they did, but he didn't consider himself any better than they were. As I look back, this was his most valuable lesson to me.

Get involved in the community. Do good things for people. Never consider yourself better than anybody else. Always have a kind word for people. Don't disparage others with words or actions. Let others feel proud of their lot in life. Be generous. Take care of the less fortunate. Have a soft heart.

Although his last days with the company were as involuntary as McArthur's were in the military, he spent them selflessly -- taking care of the customers who always took care of him. Fighting for a few extra dollars on Evian water, just like the good old days. You're not getting a gold watch from me, Dad. Your life's work deserves more than that and I'm not sure I can ever repay you. I will speak for the thousands you have touched in your lifetime, all from behind that beaten up service counter. Thanks for helping *us all* cross the finish line.

THE IMPORTANCE OF A CUSTOMER~FOCUSED VISION

It takes an obsession about customers to win business.

Have you caught the fantasy baseball bug yet? When asked to join a friend's fantasy league this year, I accepted, not *fully* knowing what was required. In fantasy baseball, players (fans) in a fictional league choose players and follow their stats during the baseball season. When their players perform well, the fantasy player's baseball team does well! I knew I was in trouble when my friend told me he had spent over 20 hours dissecting his team, position-by-position, and searching other rosters for possible trading partners. I didn't even know my team's name; let alone how to access the league's website!

Here's the point. My buddy was obsessed with fantasy baseball, and *to do something extraordinarily well, it must be your obsession.* If your goal is to cross the finish line with your customers, then the most important priority should be *articulating a customer focused vision.* In short, from top to bottom, the entire organization must be obsessed with delivering unparalleled customer service. As Janelle Barlow (2006) says in her book *Branded Customer Service – The New Competitive Advantage,* "Making customer service part of the brand has to be a strategic decision." My experiences have taught me the same lesson. It has to be more than just *lip service.*

Successful execution of customer service initiatives reduces the impact of competitors and is difficult to copy. It is simple to *want* a customer focused culture, but it certainly isn't easy to live and breathe customer service all the time or to, more importantly, make it part of the company's fiber.

Here are some important factors for articulating a customer focused vision.

- **The CEO must be obsessed** - he or she must demonstrate an unwavering commitment to the plan.

The leaders of the greatest customer service companies are obsessed with their service. Since I started this piece by talking about baseball, I should mention the Atlanta Braves baseball team. The Atlanta Braves won 14 straight division titles in an unrivaled streak that finally ended a few years ago. The Braves never had any inherent advantages over other teams. They chose their players just like the 29 other teams; however, once a player was in the fold, they became accustomed to winning. Their General Manager, John Sherholtz, was about winning and *only* winning. That is how a great leader operates.

The leader of your company can't depend on others to do the *leading*! He or she must always be monitoring the progress of the team by developing initiatives that compliment the plan, not take away from it. He must always generate pride and motivate the staff. Does the company leader expect you to say 'hello' to each customer, but then walks by everybody without saying a word? If so, he or she is sending an inconsistent message. For the initiative to be successful, the message must be consistent. Only then will it rally the troops to give great service.

Often, a company will make news when they lay off thousands of their employees while announcing a new customer service initiative. Those actions are inconsistent. A business gives better service with *more associates, not fewer*. That's just the way it works.

- **Continually discuss the vision** - companies spend an inordinately small amount of time talking about their *raison d'être (reason to be).*

Within the company, associates should always be asking, "Where are we going and what is it going to look like when we get there?" This is why the vision is so important. Without it, your associates will lack answers to their questions. They will be uncertain about how to conduct themselves.

Our vision at Sam's was spelled out in our brand promise, *"Making the experience of buying of wine and spirits as wonderful as drinking them!"* The statement was simple, but it packed a powerful punch. It was short, succinct, embraced by associates throughout the company, and easy to memorize. Since it was developed by associates at all levels, it helped align everybody in the company. All behaviors could easily be measured against this brand promise. The actions either matched the promise or didn't match the promise. It was our roadmap for improving the experience of shopping with us.

What is your *"reason to be"* in business? Certainly, the first priority is to put food on the table and to provide for life's basic necessities. Great service providers, however, peel back the layers and look deeper. Our top priority (and a responsibility I took very seriously) was to provide for the several hundred families that derived their income from our business.

When we looked deeper, we realized we also had a large hand in our customers' celebrations and milestones. There were many reasons to buy wine and spirits and many were celebratory.

For example, indirectly, we were part of many weddings, Bar Mitzvah's, 50th wedding anniversaries and summer parties. Many Bordeaux aficionados bought their first bottle of this special wine from us. As wine gets better *with age*, many customers bought wine to store for their grandchildren. We were part of many happy and significant occasions.

Other celebrations might include the achievement of a company goal or milestone. Maybe something fun such as (hopefully during my lifetime) a Chicago Cubs World Series Championship! Whatever the reason, most were happy, memorable occasions. Our goal: why not have the shopping experience match?

- **Remove the "silos"** – so everybody works together.

In many businesses, different departments (or silos) fail to communicate with each other. The result is inconsistent customer service across the organization. For example, a customer's shopping experience may be exceptional; however, if the billing clerk speaks to the customer rudely, all goodwill will be lost. To build customer loyalty, the whole company must be involved. Everybody needs to be on the same page. It is everybody's job!

It's important that associates from different departments *cross standard boundaries* and work together efficiently. Everybody needs to look at the big picture, together.

If the accounts receivable clerk shows appreciation, then the customer will remember this above anything else. What if the clerk asks the customer if they enjoyed their purchases? The customer focused vision will be reinforced in a superb way!

- **Motivate your associates** - by giving them a snapshot of the big picture.

Many companies share much more information with their associates than in the past because associates today want to know how they fit into the big picture. They want to know more about the company. They want their jobs to be more meaningful. They have questions: They want to know "How are my efforts helping the company reach its goals?" "What are the company's goals and objectives?" "How are we to measure progress towards these goals?" "What are some behaviors that will help achieve the company's goals?" Your associates want to know how *change* will help the company reach the finish line with customers. Otherwise, it is *change* for the sake of *change,* and we know how people feel about that!

It was ultimately up to my managers and me to share the reasons for our actions. When customers left our stores with full shopping carts, I asked our associates to go and retrieve the cart (as the customer was loading their purchases into their car) for no other reason than to say, "Thanks" or "Have a nice day!" I knew that even though the customer had paid and left the store, there were still opportunities to provide great service.

Often, the end of a shopping experience is what the customer remembers the most. It can be the most vivid memory of the entire shopping experience. When I enthusiastically explained that this unusual step (personally retrieving shopping carts) was driven by an obsession to serve customers properly, I received more cooperation from everybody. We made sure to carefully note how these actions tied back to our goals and objectives. The result: more buy-in! In other words, when our associates understood how their efforts helped, they were motivated and enthusiastic about taking those extra steps.

It takes commitment and an obsession with customers from everyone in the organization to be successful. It seems simple, but it certainly isn't easy to keep attention always focused on customers. After all, there are so many other tasks to accomplish. Great customer service leaders are constantly reminding everybody (including themselves) that it is the customers who pay the freight and put food on the table. When a company gets it right; however, customers are easy to attract and keep.

MANAGING CUSTOMER RELATIONSHIPS

Tracking customers' needs, and wants, leads to customer loyalty.

If you're a recreational swimmer, then you probably know there is a line on the bottom of the pool. Follow the blue line and you should get to the other end. Sadly, in open water swimming, no such line exists. Long ago, I was a recreational triathlete. The running and biking I could handle; it was the swimming that caused me fits. I wasn't so swift. Driftwood gave me a run for my money.

One year I did a triathlon in Central Florida called the "Intimidator." That was my first mistake! I should have swum as fast as I could *the other way.* As swimming is not my strong suit, after a few short minutes I was *far* behind the other swimmers. Unfortunately, I wasn't doing what I learned in open water swimming 101. Coaches teach you a technique called *tracking.* When you *track*, you look up every few strokes to see where you are going! Since I wasn't tracking, I soon found myself far *off course* in the choppy, open waters of Lake Clermont. I may have actually spotted the Gulf of Mexico.

The concept of tracking in open water swimming can teach us a valuable lesson about managing customer relationships. To be *on course* with your customers, you must constantly be looking up to see if you are going the right way and making the best moves! When we *track* our customers we find out what's important to them. We learn their likes and dislikes. We solicit their feedback. We make them feel special.

The act of communicating with customers helps nurture relationships. We placed great importance on treating our customers well. We got to know them. We developed friendships. We knew that, all things considered, people would rather do business with a friend. We became friends with our customers and we stayed in touch with them. Jeffrey Gitomer, a recognized expert on sales says, "If your customers like you, believe you, and trust you, they *may* buy from you!" Imagine if they don't like you!

Here are few things you can do to stay on track with your customers:

- **Solicit their feedback** - want to know what your customers want? Ask them!

Our customers were happy to give us their feedback and very pleased to be asked. Be sure to constantly communicate with your customers, not just the big customers, but the smaller ones also. It's true that 80% of your business probably comes from the top 20% of your customers, but you still have to communicate with everybody.

Survey your customers regularly. Do you really know what is important to them? Are your company's goals congruent with your customers' wishes? Keith Ferrazi (2006) in the book, *Never Eat Alone,* suggests that "The less you speak, the more you can hear!" Over time, we started to listen to our customers; we were surprised to learn their thoughts.

We thought our customers cared the most about price *until we asked them.* It turned out price was not their focus, and they rated great service and an expansive selection higher. Think how much money we left on the table by keeping our prices so low. Here's a tip: always give a little gift or incentive to your customer for their help. Remember, they have valuable information for you. Always thank them!

- **Market to your customer base** - spend time approaching current customers.

This is where many companies miss the boat. They spend their budgets trying to convince people to switch to them while their current and loyal customers get short changed and go elsewhere. The wireless carriers come to mind. My wireless company, instead of wanting me to change phones (upgrade) every couple of months, actually penalizes me to do so. They actively discourage an impulsive, techno-geek from spending more money in their stores. On the other hand, they spend plenty of money trying to get new customers. This is counterproductive.

Reaching customers with targeted messages is getting harder to achieve. In fact, according to the American Association of Advertising, we are inundated by thousands of marketing offers a day, yet we can only process a fraction of those messages. Spend time and money targeting your core customers. There are computer programs that will track buying habits, so it should not be difficult to know what your customers like or dislike. Use that information to get the right promotions to the right customers.

It was certainly easy and advantageous in the wine business to target loyal customers. For example, if someone had a history of buying Burgundies from us, we sent them an offering when the newest vintage of Burgundy was released. If a customer typically bought scotches between $50 and $75 per bottle, then chances were that if we had something new or special in that price range they might be interested.

In 2005, we re-engineered our marketing program. For many years, our primary tool for reaching customers and building traffic was to place ads in local newspapers. By spring of that year, we realized this was no longer the proper strategy for us. Instead, we developed a new quarterly magazine called *Pour,* and sent it to all our loyal customers. *Pour,* a 24 page magazine, featured new selections, highlighted wine growing regions and profiled innovative, cutting-edge producers. The results were increased margins, higher average tickets and *reduced* advertising expenses. It was a very successful change to our marketing mix.

There are other ways to add value. Suggest new products to customers. When new releases (or iterations) of popular products arrive, call your customers. If you can't provide a product or service, suggest another place that will accommodate their needs. I know it sounds silly; however, some of the best service stories involve sales people steering customers to other vendors if they feel they can't satisfy their needs. The fruits of such labor will be appreciative customers. What customers see is that you are trying to help them solve their problems, which is exactly what you want them to see. You've added value and, in turn, you will receive more loyalty in return.

My salesman at Nordstrom's knows exactly what brand of dress shirts I prefer and calls me when new colors come out. I love it even though I know his ultimate goal is to increase *his* commissions. It doesn't matter to me. It's a win-win situation for everybody!

- **Learn more about your customers** - get to know them as intimately as possible.

I am always amazed how much you can find out about customers by asking something as simple as *"How was your summer?"* Ask that question or something similar and you'll find out about your customer's summer vacation or maybe what camp their children attended. I never went to overnight camp but now that my contemporaries and I have children that age, all I ever hear is people comparing their ancient camping tales. Do your customers have children in college? Ask what college they are giving their life savings to for tuition, books, and fees. Maybe you went to the same college. These are connections, and connections make bonds with your customers.

People love to talk about themselves. We love to hear our names. We want to be the center of attention. How does it feel when you call a business and they recognize your voice? It's a good feeling! All things considered, people want to do business with a friend. In fact, most people are not as trusting of other people as they are of a friend. Is this important? Yes, getting to know your customers is good business.

According to a NY Times/ CBS News poll, when your customers think you "know them personally," most (88%) think you will be fair with them. Perception is reality. Let people know you, and get to know them. My Dad was great at this. By uttering the following simple words, "He's okay, I know him," my dad could truly make the difference with the customer. He could make customers feel welcome like no other.

- **Don't stop at satisfied customers** – create loyal customers.

Strive for more than just *satisfied customers*, because they only feel so-so about doing business with you. They may refer customers to you, but probably not. They may be happy, or even satisfied, with you, but feel no other emotions. The opposite is what you want to attract. Jeffrey Gitomer (1998), talks about loyal customers, in his book *Customer Satisfaction is Worthless*. "The goal is loyal customers; ones whose needs were met and exceeded." These customers have had a memorable experience and now have a great overall feeling about your company!

I realize that it's simple, but not easy, to stay on course with your customers. It's simple to talk about maintaining contact with valued customers, but not easy to actually keep doing it on a consistent basis. If the goal is to reach the finish line with your customers, then you have to be able to survive the middle miles.

Keep soliciting feedback, keep targeting and getting to know your current customers. Always be appreciative and realize that the goal is to have customers come back *a second time!* That's the true measure of a happy customer. Continue making the little things count. Before long, you will be effectively managing customer relationships. Me, I'm going to the swimming pool. Don't worry! I'm won't take my eyes off that blue line!

GREETING CUSTOMERS SINCERELY

Start every customer conversation with a warm greeting.

Nothing can start a successful experience off on the right foot like a warm greeting. For that reason, I'll always remember Melanie. Who was Melanie? She wasn't my first girlfriend. My wife, Jill, was my first girlfriend, and my second, and ...well, you get the picture. Melanie wasn't my 7th grade English teacher either. That unfortunate task went to Mrs. Jonestup, who faithfully tried teaching me grammar, while I stared out the window.

Melanie was my server on a recent trip to the California Pizza Kitchen. She smiled the entire time my banker friend and I were having lunch. Despite the fact that he and I seldom agree on much (we last agreed on what color pen we should use to sign our loan documents), on this we reached instant accord: *Melanie's smile truly made us feel welcome.*

The greeting is the proverbial *moment of truth* in many service situations. Often, it determines whether you get off on the right foot or the wrong foot with a customer. Too often, we make our customers feel unwelcome by greeting them with poker faces. We take our time greeting them, preferring, instead, to finish our current tasks; consequently, we make them feel like an interruption when we should, in fact, be thrilled that they have chosen to call us instead of our competition.

I'm sure most would agree that it takes a great degree of effort to reverse a negative first impression. Talk about heavy lifting. In *The*

Power of Nice, Linda Kaplan Thaler and Robin Koval (2006) say, "Positive impressions are like seeds. You don't see the effect right away." This is especially true of first impressions, which lay the groundwork for the entire service experience. It's just easier and wiser to do it right the first time.

Follow these four sure-fire ways to make customers comfortable and cross the finish line ahead of the competition.

- **Smile** - Melanie had a heavenly smile that made us feel welcome.

Ask my wife. I'm not the type to remember the little details. After 20 plus years together, she still insists I don't know the color of her eyes. With Melanie, however, I will not soon forget the little detail of how welcome I felt at the restaurant that day due to her genuine, warm smile. Is a smile important? It certainly is. It's why I asked Jill (my wife) out back in high school.

My high school years weren't the most romantic of times. Cross country runners weren't exactly considered the most eligible bachelors. By the end of senior year, though, I was determined to *actually* attend a school dance before I matriculated on to college. I narrowed the field down to three girls. Which one would be so lucky (unlucky)? As decision time neared, the whole school waited on pins and needles. My decision was to ask Jill to the prom. Why? I asked her because she was the one always smiling at me. Her smile made me feel welcome; made me feel important.

The same is true with our customers. A proper welcome makes our customers feel important. Always greet people with a pleasant smile. Today, in a specialty clothing store, Jill and I were greeted by a young lady chomping on a piece of gum like it was the last stick of gum on the face of the Earth! Not a great first impression! Remember the little things because customers have a habit of seeing, and remembering, the most microscopic details!

- **Be enthusiastic** - people have the weight of the world on their shoulders.

Customers, as well as many others, are short of time and stressed out. When they communicate with us or shop in our stores, they bring the sum of their cumulative experiences with our company and all the other companies they patronize. Maybe they had a bad experience with our business in the past and they're giving us a second chance. Sometimes, customers are just having a bad day all around.

In Phillip Van Hauser's book (2005) *Willie's Way: 6 Secrets to Wooing, Wowing and Winning Customers and their Loyalty*, the author says "Never expect the customer to speak first. To hesitate, even briefly, may make you appear aloof, pretentious or unapproachable in the eyes of the customer!" An enthusiastic, timely greeting will remove all doubt. Enthusiastically let the customer know you are happy to see him. It can be very disarming. If done properly, it can set the tone for the entire encounter.

My Dad had quite a way to do this. In our flagship store we had a basketball hoop up on the wall. He was an old basketball jock who loved to regale us with tales of his basketball past. When customers would enter, he would often challenge them to a *free throw* shooting contest for big discounts. He rarely lost the game or the opportunity to bond with a new customer and typically gave a generous discount anyway. I always knew the game was on when I saw the mops and smelled the wine from an errant shot or two. My dad knew how important it was to bond with and enthusiastically greet customers.

- **Make body language positive** – it's more than just what you say.

Actually, *what you say* comprises only a small part of your message. Other cues have more influence on how people are made to feel. Gestures, facial expressions and body movements play a big part. Maintaining eye contact is very important. A greeting without eye contact is superficial, and we lose a moment in time to connect with a customer.

We've all gone in a store where a clerk in the back has shouted from the back, "Hello". How hard would it be to come up front, smile, and greet us properly? Do your associates stand with their arms folded when customers are near? Do they walk the other way when customers approach? Do they congregate near one another creating an intimidating wall for customers to breech? They might as well have a "Do Not Disturb" sign hanging around their necks! Greetings must be *sincere* to make a meaningful impression.

Think about the last running race you entered or watched. Picture the crowd. Some spectators might have been saying *"nice race"* and others may have been shouting *"nice race"* while waving their hands, smiling and jumping up and down. Which spectator would you rather see with a half mile to go? Although both are saying the same thing, one method just feels better. I'm not suggesting that we yell, "The finish is right around the corner" when customers walk past; however, we should always check our body language and make sure we're making a positive impression.

- **Engage your customers** - get them talking.

Ask questions requiring more than a yes or no answer. Strike up a conversation. Learn more about your customers. It's simple, but not easy. It's simple to say "hello", but not easy to engage in dialog that requires some thought or preparation. Here's an example. In the wine business, if we see someone looking at the cabernets, we can say one of two things.

a) *Can I help you find something?*
b) *What is your favorite Cabernet?*

The first question will elicit a yes or no answer. The customer will probably say, "No." The second question will start a conversation. Let's say the customer responds by talking about a small vineyard from Napa Valley (California's very well-known wine growing region.) We could use that information to suggest a similar cabernet from Sonoma, another wine growing region not far from Napa Valley.

Want to really impress the customer? Explain how Napa and Sonoma cabernets are similar, and how they are different. That's called adding value and sharing passion for your products. Keep teaching your customers and sharing your enthusiasm. Get them involved in the process. If you are showing your customer a bottle, let your customer hold it. Let them *feel and touch* the product. I don't know about you, but when I pick up a tie at Nordstrom, I usually buy it. Typically, the customer will rarely put the item back on the shelf once it is in their hands.

Keep engaging the customer with great eye contact. Keep asking questions. Keep teaching and educating. Before you know it, a new relationship will be forming.

- **Make customers feel comfortable** – in uncomfortable surroundings

One reason a greeting is so important is because it reduces stress. Entering new and different environments poses an anxious situation for some customers and clients. After all, they are entering unfamiliar territory. Our workplaces are familiar to us because we go there every day. Think how we feel when we go to the home of someone we don't know very well. Usually, we're pretty shy until the host greets us warmly. The same is true in our stores and offices.

All things considered, people would rather do business with a friend, so it's best to start building relationships. Like it or not, customers size us up with those initial impressions. To borrow a phrase from famous restaurateur, *Danny Meyer*, the first few moments *set the table* for the rest of the service experience. Get off on the wrong foot, and it's very hard to recover. Thanks to Melanie, patrons at the California Pizza Kitchen feel welcome.

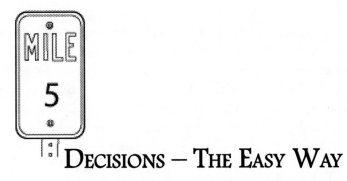

Decisions – The Easy Way

Be honest, ethical, and prepared and make the right decisions.

I didn't go there to pick up hardware or for the fame and thrill of victory. I simply wanted to run a local race with some of my friends so one warm Sunday morning we toed the line at the *Deerfield Dash 5k and 10k*. Not quite the World Championships but hey, there was a free T-shirt. It was a recreational crowd to say the least. Lots of children, people running with dogs, etc. There weren't many serious runners in the crowd and my running hat, cool shades and elaborate (but extremely ineffective) stretching routine probably set me apart. I was ready!

The race started and holy cow, guess what place I'm in? Yes, I am in the lead. First place! A position I've never been in -- right behind the police car! I never even won a race in high school. I came in second, *once*, (yes, there were more than 2 runners!) but never crossed the finish line before anybody else. Could this be the day? Could I be destined for *Deerfield Dash* greatness? Was I going to be forever immortalized in the winner's circle -- somebody locals would talk about for years to come? After a while the course separated. The police car continued on the 10K route and I turned onto the 5K course. I was all alone. Not another runner in sight. That's when the trouble started.

I had reached the proverbial fork in the road, a four way intersection with no signs. I felt like Dorothy on the yellow brick road but I didn't have the scarecrow to tell me which way to go. I went the wrong way. Why? I have no idea. When I reached the pivotal point, instead of simply going straight, I turned despite the lack of any signs *actually* telling me to turn. In retrospect, I simply over-thought the situation.

Has that ever happened to you? Have you ever had something so close you could taste it, but then did something stupid and blew it? Why does this happen? Why do we over-think things? Perhaps we want so much to do the right thing that we can't, from time to time, see the forest for the trees.

Reaching the finish line with your customers isn't rocket science. However, it does require that you don't suffer paralysis by analysis. I once read a quote by Jim Kaat, a former major league baseball pitcher. *"If you think too long, you think wrong."* I was probably guilty of that in the race! Make the right decisions for the right reasons and things will be fine. Everyone can cross the finish line with their customers; but you have to have good decision making skills.

Here are a few things to keep in mind:

- **Prepare for success** – Have a plan for your customer relationships.

If I had studied the course map, I never would have deliberated what to do at that intersection. Part of being successful with your customers is preparation. Woody Allen once said, "90% of success is showing up." Jeffrey Gitomer, author of many wonderful business books, adds that "Not only do you have to show up, but you have to be prepared!" Carefully plan how each interaction should go. Be prepared with what you might do in various situations. There is no such thing as being too prepared. Consider all the possibilities and have the appropriate responses. This way, when you reach the fork in the road, you will instinctively know what to do.

- **Never cross the line of ethical behavior** – always be honest.

Never compromise your values or your company's values. If your company condones unethical behavior, then you should get a new job. As a retail business owner, I often saw examples of dishonest behavior. I dealt with those situations swiftly and decisively. One time, a manager was overcharging and cheating unsuspecting customers out of a few pennies. He was relieved of his command immediately.

When customers have placed their trust in us, violations of such confidence are the ultimate betrayal. If you're unsure what to do, follow the simple rule: *When in doubt, don't do it.* Still unsure, follow this golden rule! *Don't do to others what you don't want done to you.* I used to caution our associates: when we're honest, we don't have to remember what we said. We can't *get caught* in anything because the truth will come out naturally. Play by the rules and decisions will be easier to make successfully.

- **Be fair with your customers** – fairness will pay dividends.

Fairness is crucial, especially when dealing with customer complaints. When things go wrong, some customers complain. It's actually a good thing! Most dissatisfied people stop being your customers and never tell you. They simply shop somewhere else.

Accordingly, when people do complain, do the right thing for them. Ask how you can make things right. If their method for resolving the situation is fair, just do it. Keep the customer. Has a business ever cast you away for what seems like pennies? It actually happens all the time! Businesses cast away their most precious commodities because of a very small disagreement. Over and over, I've learned that when we're fair with a customer, he or she will actually want less than what we were willing to give them to resolve the problem.

How did the *Deerfield Dash* end up? After a few minutes of running the wrong way, I got a sinking feeling that something was amiss. *Houston, we have a problem!* I finally re-joined the course in time to come in 5th or 6th place. The exact place, I don't remember clearly, but I do remember being nudged out by a man pushing his twins *in a baby jogger.* Of all the indignity! What a stunning fall from grace.

Be fair, honest, ethical, prepared and confident and decisions will be much easier to make. As for me, I have to go. The inaugural Riverwoods 5k (a picturesque race around my neighborhood) is starting soon. I've stacked the deck in my favor. It's me and my children. I'll *see you* on top of the awards podium!

WHEN CUSTOMERS DON'T SPEAK UP

Listen to and act upon customer feedback.

I imagine you've all had experiences like this. You hear about a swank new restaurant, the kind that's booked solid for the next 6 months. Undeterred, you gamely pick up the phone, make a reservation, and file it away in the back of your calendar - *next year's calendar!* On the appointed day, you arrive 5 minutes early only to be seated *30 minutes* late. To make matters worse, once you're seated, it takes *forever* to bring menus, cocktails, appetizers, etc.

Then the dishes come out wrong. You ordered the pasta primavera, but the waiter brings chicken parmesan. Your spouse's dish looks as if it was cooked *that morning*. The whole thing is an unmitigated disaster. I imagine we've all had at least one of these experiences in our dining lifetimes! To be sure, with so much to do, operating a restaurant must be a great challenge.

The interesting part is what happens next. As you and your friends are lamenting the terrible service and experience, the manager strolls over, seemingly oblivious to the mayhem unfolding before him. Cheerfully, he extends his hand and bellows, "How is everything tonight?" On cue, as if he is choreographing your every move, almost controlling your thoughts, you respond, "Everything is fine, thank you!"

Have you ever had an awful, ridiculous experience in a restaurant, or store, or on the phone, and when questioned about your experience answered that way? Have you responded that everything was great when, in fact, it was *quite the opposite?* It has happened to me more times than I care to admit.

We want customers to give us their honest opinions. Customers who hide their true feelings are the kiss of death for service providers. They have terrible experiences, but for some reason, are reluctant to speak up when questioned. To cross the finish line with your customers you must first understand why people don't complain more often, and develop strategies to bring out their feedback.

Is this important? Yes! There are few pieces of the customer service puzzle that are more crucial than getting customers to voice their displeasure! Many studies show that only a miniscule 2-4% of customers will actually take the time and effort to complain. Most simply go elsewhere. They vote with their feet by walking out your side door while you are desperately trying to get people to come through the front door.

Here are a few reasons why customers don't complain and what you can do to alleviate their concerns.

- **They think you don't care** - show them you do care.

Head off customer complaints at the pass. Make it easy! Customers who take the time and effort to let their feelings be known are actually saying (no, SHOUTING) "I want to be your customer. Do something!" They are giving you a second chance, an opportunity to show how great you can really be! Show them that their opinions won't fall upon deaf ears.

- **They're afraid of a confrontation** - handle things professionally.

Never argue with your customers. Arguing with a customer is a situation that typically ends with two losers: (1) they will lose face if you embarrass them, especially in front of others, and (2) you will lose a customer. It's simple, but not easy to keep your cool! Simple to get into heated discussions with customers, but not easy to take the high road and steer clear of such situations.

In the wine business, customers often bring back *bad* bottles of wine. I once had a manager who would give customers returning a *bad* bottle of wine the third degree, right in front of everybody. He would call over a wine guru to take a quick taste of the bottle. Sometimes, the wine was actually corked (in other words, defective), and other times the customer was simply mistaken or not used to the taste. How do you think they felt during this Spanish inquisition? Humiliated? They probably felt violated on many levels. Trying the wine in front of the customer was tantamount to saying, *"You don't know how this wine should taste and we know it!"* Those exchanges never ended well.

In such cases, it was much more prudent to take the bottle back right away. We found it best to have a *no questions asked* policy! We were never going to win those battles. Robert Bacal (2005) makes a similar point in his book *Perfect Phrases for Customer Service*. "The goal in a situation like this is to find agreement points. Sometimes, a simple "You're right!" will help diffuse the situation." That approach surprises an angry customer. Often, they won't know what to say next, which allows you to equitably handle the situation.

- **They think you don't want to hear feedback** - ask for it.

Show your customers you want their feedback by asking for it. A simple statement like "How can we improve our service?" will work wonders with your customer base. Ken Blanchard (2004) in *Customer Mania* suggests the following simple questions: "How can we make the experience better?" and "What can we do to provide better service?"

Another revealing question is "What should we do that we are not currently doing?" Generally, customers will share this information with you. You may get clues on product and service trends which may tell you what customers will be expecting 1 year from now. The goal is to encourage customers to be specific and to get them to start talking! Surveys have become very easy and economical to circulate. Poll your customers about the top three to five things they would like to see changed or fixed and act upon that list immediately. Have a thick skin and fish for negative feedback! That's how you improve your business. Let your customers know that, with their input, you will be able to provide them with better service.

- **They think you won't do anything about it** - show them that is not the case.

Your challenge is to act immediately, and to develop strategies to counteract this perception. Once customers see some action, they will happily give you their honest feedback.

I remember a situation with a customer who took the time to write me an email. This gentleman called our store multiple times, and did not receive a return call, all over a minor billing error. He was justifiably upset when we spoke, but when my associates and I professionally corrected his problem, the paradigm shifted. He was now **thanking me**! That's what happens when you take customer complaints seriously. My experience in all my years of delighting customers is that once you deal with a customer's problem in a professional manner, you will have much more loyalty than ever before. Typically, all parties involved will forget what the problem was to begin with. That's great news!

Let's go back to the terrible restaurant experience. The manager should have known there was a disaster unfolding at table 16. Encourage your customers to give honest feedback. When they do, take it seriously. For you restaurateurs out there, please, please seat me promptly. I have an early bedtime.

Business Etiquette 101

Put customers at ease and they will come back.

Is anyone familiar with the one-tooth purple dinosaur? His name is Barney and through his books, my children and I have gone to the fire station, the dentist, and of course, the library. Most importantly, we've all learned basic manners from the best seller *"Barney Says Please and Thank You!"* For many years, every night before bed, our children would learn great manners from Barney.

Am I suggesting that we learn business lessons from a children's book? Not exactly, but there are a few things we can glean from this classic tome. Good manners put customers at ease, and comfortable customers come back again and again. Crossing the finish line with customers is no easy task. Customer relationships usually start out positively, but things change as customers continue to walk through our doors. What changes? They scrutinize us more. Inevitably, as the bloom falls off the rose, customers start looking for the reasons why they give us their business. It's almost as if they have to justify it, both to their friends and themselves.

Take a lesson from the world of marathon running. As you can imagine, it's important to eat nutritiously when logging lots of miles. It's wise to eat cereals rich in iron. Unfortunately, your body absorbs this muscle-repairing nutrient slowly. Add some strawberries and you double the absorption rates. For some reason, ingesting vitamin C helps the body absorb more iron. Here's the connection, and the reason for the dietary advice. All the little things we do to show our customers we value them are helpful. Individually, insightful actions build the foundation of great service. Start layering these positive touch points, one on top of another, and customers start to notice. The effect will be exponential. Your customers will feel more appreciated and wanted. Most importantly, they won't feel neglected.

You can accomplish these things in so many ways:

- **Do the little things** – the devil is in the details.

Open the door for a customer, or hold it. Find a chair for someone who is waiting. Better yet, escort them to the chair instead of pointing your finger. Have a clean store and parking lot. Want to make the ladies feel special? Give out flowers on Mother's day. Anticipate your customer's needs. Be aware of customers and approach them. Don't wait for them to approach you. Be customer advocates.

I had the privilege in business for many years to witness literally thousands of selfless customer-focused acts for the benefit of our customers. Over and over, I saw our associates anticipating customer needs and acting quickly. Sometimes, it was saving a customer by bringing a shopping cart to them. Other times it was going above and beyond to make a delivery on time! I loved seeing an associate taking extra time to describe the qualities of a particular wine selection to a confused customer. Sometimes, it was the act of finding a way to bring a special wine into the market for a customer. I considered these acts going the extra mile.

Sometimes, companies go above and beyond to surprise customers. The other day, Blue Cross Blue Shield, the mammoth health insurance carrier, helped my buddy with an insurance issue. Seems there was a problem with the way the doctor was handling his claim paperwork. Blue Cross expedited a solution by communicating with the doctor on his behalf. To be sure, companies like Blue Cross can easily neglect their customers. Who are their customers, anyway? Is it the company sponsoring the health plan, or the patient?

Patients certainly have little say in the matter. If you don't like your health insurance, your choices are *no insurance,* or to find *an individual carrier.* Neither are inspiring choices, to say the least! Companies like Blue Cross are undoubtedly more successful by surprising their customers with more service, rather than indifferent, undistinguished service.

- **Take care of the children** – always welcome the little ones.

What happens when our children are kept occupied while we are shopping? We get more time to shop. How does that affect retailers? Numerous studies (and my own independent research with my three boys) have shown that the longer consumers stay in stores, the more they will buy. It's all about keeping the little ones happy.

Often, but not nearly enough, we would give balloons away to little boys and girls. Someone once asked me what kind of work-related things I did on Saturdays? I can tell you what I *enjoyed* doing. I enjoyed handing out balloons. One of my happiest moments in business was seeing the wonderful smile that resulted from the simple act of tying a balloon around a child's wrist.

My Dad loved to point out the security TV monitors to children as they would enter. He would say, "I knew you'd be a TV star!" The children loved to see themselves on TV, and we loved that their parents had *plenty* of time to shop. It was a win-win situation for everybody.

- **Keep it clean** – maintain a professional environment.

Have you seen High School Musical 1 or 2? No, I don't have a crush on Troy. Well, maybe just a small one. I really love those movies. The singing, dancing and acting is great, especially as the cast is so young. The music is catchy! The interesting thing is the script. In this era of skin, violence, and profanity, it's nice to see the Disney Company produce such successful hits that don't rely on the usual evocative ingredients of many movies. The stars, Troy and Gabriella, don't even kiss until the end of the sequel. It is clean, wholesome, and very professionally done.

Maintain a professional atmosphere at all times. Avoid inappropriate conversation. How your associates act, how they dress, and how they conduct themselves are all important success factors. It was always challenging, during the hot summers of Chicago, to expect our associates to dress appropriately, especially if we were trying to save on the air conditioning bill!

Have you ever been in the checkout line while the cashier is carrying on an animated conversation on his or her cell phone? It feels lousy to be neglected like that. Keep profanity out of your establishment. Always keep disagreements between associates away from customers. It's unsettling for customers to see your associates arguing, and possibly fighting, in the middle of the workplace. Remember, you can have all the fancy people and systems in the world at the corporate office; however, the front line people are who the customers see as the face of the company. Keep things professional at all times.

Never yell at your associates in front of customers. For that matter, never yell at your associates; it can be very upsetting. Try not to say things you might later regret. Remember the words of the infamous author unknown. *"Not even the fastest horse can catch a word spoken in anger!"* Take difficult conversations behind closed doors. Keep the stores clean. Keep the bathrooms clean. Wear clean uniforms.

Professional services firms: make sure your receptionist behaves and dresses properly. Think this isn't important? The receptionist is usually the first person people see when they come to your office. Remember, comfortable customers will be repeat customers. Never forget your business etiquette.

Remember to appreciate your customers with good manners long after they are gone and the sale is complete. They will show their appreciation by continuing to be your customer, by coming back again and again, and that should be enough motivation for all of us.

RESPECTING TIME AND INTELLIGENCE

Prepare to handle customer's needs before they arrive.

Do you ever wonder if the company you do business with respects your intelligence? Think they care how much time you spend trying to buy their goods or services? Let's face it; there is no shortage of ways (and places) to spend your money. An abundance of choices exists around us, much more than in our parent's generation. Of course, at the airport, there aren't as many choices, especially at the security checkpoints.

The other day I arrived at O'Hare for a 6 a.m. flight. It was a Thursday, and the beginning of the long Labor Day weekend, so there were plenty of passengers, most rubbing their eyes at that early hour. The line stretched on and on, because there was only one checkpoint open. Most lanes were closed at that hour. I started to think how the TSA doesn't have to be concerned with customer service, or how long passengers have to wait in line. Short of buying their own planes, their customers don't have other alternatives.

Whether you operate a law firm, a retail store or a manufacturing facility, your customers have choices and alternatives. Your customer's time has become scarce. Everybody is always running full speed to catch a flight or pick up the kids at soccer practice. The demands on time are endless. Companies that survive the middle miles and cross the finish line with their customers truly understand the role respect plays in the customer service equation.

Keep the following in mind and customers will feel you're respecting their time and intelligence:

- **Concentrate on the important things** – keep the frills to a minimum.

Do you ever go to the post office around lunchtime? That's a pleasant experience! Usually, there are lots of people waiting and one or two people working behind the counter. Reminds me of a story I heard recently. The NY Times has a diary they call the Metropolitan Journal. Readers write in with their personal experiences. One told of a trip to the post office. There were 20 or more people in line and one person working behind the counter. Some customers had been waiting over 30 minutes and patience was starting to thin.

Suddenly, five postal employees appeared carrying a ladder, balloons and a sign. They hung the sign, which said *Customer Appreciation Week*! Seeing this, one postal patron approached and said, "Do you see the inconsistency here. Some people in this line have been waiting 30 minutes. You have one person working behind the counter and now you come hang a sign that says this?" The gentleman looked up at the sign and said, *"Oh, the sign….that doesn't start until next week!"*

In our business we realized that it's the little things that keep people coming back again and again, not the frills. We always had enough people on the floor, on the phone, and available for customers. We also knew that having plenty of cashiers was a great ingredient for success. We realized that nothing ruined a great experience as much as having to wait in line to pay. To reduce the likelihood of this happening, we staffed accordingly. It was a small, but unique, point of differentiation.

Winning companies realize that providing exceptional service requires an investment. To be sure, there were many times when I thought we had too many associates. Sometimes, while sitting in rush hour traffic going home from work, I would ponder how much money we could save by having less people on the floor. I resisted the urge, and when there was a surge in shoppers, we were ready. In the post office story above, special promotions like commemorative stamps and "Customer Appreciation Weeks" are nice, but what customers really want is to spend less time trying to mail a letter on their lunch hour.

- **Have what your customer's want** - when they want it.

Have the right products on hand. Our wine stores had massive inventories. Was this the right way to run a business? Sometimes I wondered. There was a great opportunity cost inherent in tying up money in inventory. However, from the time I started in the business, my dad taught me a valuable lesson. He told me to always have what the customers want. He knew that if a customer wanted something and we didn't have it, they would go somewhere else. When you don't have what your customers' want, why should they come to you? What do they need you for? They'll just go somewhere else.

The dilemma with inventory levels: when is enough, enough? Ever wonder where to draw the line? Many businesses fail because they substitute *having everything* for *having the right things*. Neil Stern and Willard Ander (2004) in their book, *Winning at Retail,* state that "Stocking everything is a disservice to your customer. It creates too many choices and makes it difficult for customers to find what they want." Invest the time and money to find the right products. To keep abreast of changes in the wine business, we would send people to Europe and the western part of the United States to learn the latest wine trends. We would sponsor wine events to see what customers were enjoying. We asked for their feedback!

We made sure to have our order and replenishment systems in top shape so the top products were on hand at the right times. It wasn't enough to have a wide selection of gewürztraminers, but we needed to have the right bottle of Gewurztraminer when our customer stopped by on a Tuesday morning or a Thursday evening!

The Internet has raised the ante even more. Nowadays, if you don't need something right away, you can order it with just a few mouse clicks. Internet merchants don't have the same costs as brick and mortar retailers, which complicates things even more. They can source goods in different ways. In the late 1990's, some experts predicted that everything was going to be purchased online, and that traditional retail was going to be less important.

That obviously didn't happen. A few Internet retailers survived, the rest disappeared and regular businesses are still around. Why? Because customers want what they want, when they want it. They want to touch things and to feel things. Many like the human interaction. Be sure to have the right products on hand.

- **Make it easy for your customers** - to do business with you.

Have enough people answering the phones. Make sure products can be reached easily by your customers. Fix the problems sooner, rather than later. I learned something in running marathons that applies here. I'd be running a race and feel a little pebble in my shoe, or the laces on my shoes would become untied. Typically, I'd keep going while the little voice in my head told me to stop, take a few moments, and correct the problem. Was it worth 30 seconds to take my shoe off, shake it, and put it back on? Yes! It would probably save 15 miles of blister induced pain later on!

The same holds true in business. Just like that little pebble wasn't going anywhere on its own, problems in your operation and inefficiencies in your company are not going to correct themselves. Fix what is broken. Anticipate your customers' needs. Study their habits. Watch how they interact with your staff and how they order your products.

Here's an example: At our wines stores, many customers bought multiple cases of wine. They needed help out to their car. Sometimes, another customer would be unpacking their trunk with things they planned to return. The question was always do we wait for the customer to come into the store asking for help or do we instinctively go help them first? We taught our associates to be proactive. To see a simple situation like that as an opportunity to approach the customer with an offer of assistance. We weren't necessarily creating a memorable experience; but a meaningful encounter. With each meaningful gesture, though, we inched closer to creating a memorable experience. Respecting our customer's time and anticipating their needs were big parts of the equation.

Do you ask your associates what they see? Do you ask them to help identify other opportunities to create meaningful touch points? You should! Your front line associates are bursting to share their knowledge with you. They want to provide good service.

Encourage your associates to show some initiative. Yesterday, a few colleagues and I had a quick breakfast in a restaurant. We were in a hurry. The server, knowing this, brought our check with the food.

That displayed a little initiative. He was able to size up the situation and act accordingly. He accommodated our needs. Not rocket science, to be sure, but he was respecting our time.

Always make sure to respect your customer's time and intelligence. Concentrate on the little things that make shopping difficult and fix those things immediately. Trust me; if *you* can easily identify *what's broken*, your customers (or former customers) have already seen the same things. They're probably giving their business to someone else now! Worse yet, they never even said goodbye. Hopefully, they're not taking their friends and family with them.

How To Avoid The Curse Of Complacency

Are you asking the right questions?

I understand the concept of complacency. Been there and done that. Complacency, according to the dictionary, is being pleased with oneself or one's merits, advantages, and situation, often without awareness of potential danger. Have you ever been complacent? Have you ever been very happy with a situation, only to realize later that things weren't really so great? It's been my experience in many years of business that at one time or another, all businesses fall into the complacency trap and as the song goes, *"You never realize what you have until it's gone."*

My memory of the family business stretches back more than 25 years. I remember times when things were great, and I couldn't imagine they would ever be different. Former tennis star Rod Laver once said, *"The time your game is most vulnerable is when you're ahead. Never let up!"* It's not that we let up, but our situation was slowly changing. For starters, the competitive landscape was transforming. Costco arrived with a flourish on the wine and spirit scene. They shortly became the number one seller of wine and spirits in the U.S. They had a profound impact on the fortunes of independent retailers.

At the same time, costs for virtually everything were going up across the board. Insurance premiums (post 9/11) went through the roof.

Other expense categories like real estate taxes, health insurance, and workers compensation premiums were all increasing as well. It became more challenging to run the business the way we had in the past.

We fought through our "complacency" stage, and you can too! Ask the right questions and seek answers you may not necessarily want. Read the following eight questions, and start protecting your company from the evils of complacency. Remember, to cross the finish line, you have to *stay in the race!* Ask the tough questions. The results will be a healthy, continuing business with happy customers and happy associates.

- **Are your gross margins going up or down?** What goes down doesn't necessarily go back up.

When your margins fall, you may be unwittingly training your customers to expect lower prices. You then run the risk of having alienated or disappointed customers when you try to raise prices again. Keep your margins as constant as you can, unless, of course, keeping them low will force you out of business. That only helps your competitors! Remember, your customers are creatures of habit. They don't like change. They want things to be the same. Keep things constant for them.

- **Are you trying to be all things to all people?** Don't try to do too much!

The old adage when a business closes its doors is, "We were busy until the very end!" If you are really busy, but aren't making any money, then your prices may be too low. My favorite ads are the ones that say "Price, Service, and Selection." We used to say that, but in this day and age, it's extremely difficult to run a business that way. Pick two out of the three and get to work. Are your prices higher than your competitors? Make sure you are giving a much higher level of service and selection.

Several years ago, Inc Magazine (June, 2001) called Green Hills Farm "The best little grocery store in America." The accompanying story mentioned that Green Hill's CEO Gary Hawkins believes that the frozen turkey is a symbol of all that's wrong with the bloated marketing habits of the grocery-store industry in which he competes. Specifically, he has a bone to pick with grocers who use the turkey to reward the thieves, that is, the bargain-thirsty, store-hopping, emotionally-unable-to-commit customers who methodically sweep into a store, spend a few bucks, and walk out with the big prize: a free or nearly free Thanksgiving turkey. Green Hill's philosophy: *don't be all things to all people.* Target the customers that will *actually* help your business.

- **Do your associates still like coming to work?** What is the mood within your company?

Convene a focus group or have an informal internet survey. There are more and more inexpensive ways to get your associates' opinions, if you want them. Create and maintain an environment where your associates *feel* they can speak freely. Take the top three concerns your associates have about your company and fix them. At the very least, use the good times to throw some value their way. Let them know and feel that the success the company is enjoying is due to them. Let them have some credit! Having the right atmosphere in good times will help if things start going the other way.

- **How does your business look?** Is it time for some renovations or general upkeep?

What has wear and tear done to your facilities? Don't look at this yourself. Have someone else give you an honest assessment because they will spot things that you either won't see or won't admit seeing! Throw a fresh coat of paint up every once in a while. Customers will enjoy that, and your associates will as well. Are your bathrooms clean? Don't lose sight of the little details.

The other day my wife was out grocery shopping with our son Ben, when suddenly, as 4-year olds do, he announced the need for a bathroom. The woman's bathroom was occupied so they ventured into the men's. It was disgusting, and this was from a small chain known by all for its excellent customer service. Part of crossing the finish line with your customers and associates is meeting their tangible needs. Tangible needs can mean different things to different people. In this case, it meant a clean bathroom for Ben!

- **Can you improve your systems?** Are you getting the right information from your systems?

Don't settle for your systems giving you the right information now. Plan ahead! What other information is available? Can your checkout process be more efficient, or quicker? Our wine stores did a big telephone business and we used to take many orders over the phone. One day the software was changed to allow us to easily access customer purchasing history while the associate was on the phone with the customer. Wow, a new selling opportunity right before our eyes and source of information to help us provide great service. Always be thinking of what the system should do tomorrow, not what it is doing today.

- **Are you gaining or losing customers?** Are you doing everything you can to retain customers?

Are you adding more clients? Are your annual clients signing on for next year? If not, what are their reasons for leaving? Are your transaction counts going up or down? How about the average ticket? Declining average tickets can be a sign that your associates aren't being attentive enough. Paco Underhill (2004) in his book, *Why People Buy*, proves through numerous research studies that, "The longer someone stays in your store, the more they will purchase." Are you keeping customers in the stores long enough?

- **Do you know your best customers?** Do you communicate with them regularly?

Communicate, not just when they've just bought something, but also, just for the sake of open communication and friendliness. Dale Carnegie (1936), in his legendary book *How to Win Friends and Influence People,* teaches that the greatest sound in the English language is the sound of your own name. While times are good, are you getting to know your customers better?

One day, I called our best customer out of the blue. He was thrilled. He started telling me what a great operation we had. It was very gratifying. He was touched that we reached out to him, and he started doing more business with us. Our relationship was strengthened. Always remember that all things considered, people would rather do business with their friends.

- **Are your associates becoming more knowledgeable?** What role does training play in your company?

Is educating your associates an afterthought? The brand promise at our wine stores was very simple: "To make the experience of buying wines and spirits as wonderful as drinking them!" To live up to this promise, we needed training year around. According to an article published by the American Management Association, *You Can't Build a Brand without Your Employees,* "managers should never automatically assume that associates understand the brand strategy." They suggest always taking extra time to reinforce that brand message.

We took this to heart. Our associates became more knowledgeable than our competitors' associates because we trained them more. We took it very seriously. We used training as a motivator. Part of hiring, motivating, and retaining the best employees is for them to feel a sense of ownership and growth. Training helps accomplish this, which in turn, helps the company hold on to its best people.

Typically, companies focus on top-line growth when business is going well. The talk is *more* about how much revenues are increasing, instead of what is happening to the bottom line. Eye-popping growth is simply more interesting than the fundamentals.

The Gap clothing stores are a great case in point. Their first store opened in 1969 and they had a great run for many years. Unfortunately, things have gone south the last 10 years. The company expanded like crazy with Old Navy, Banana Republic and all the other Gap brands (Gap Kids and Gap Body, etc.). Many believe that the Gap didn't stay true to what *brought them to the dance.* They missed badly in the mid to late 90's with their fashion picks, and they've never been the same. Now they are returning to their core, but it may be too late to reverse the damage. *Always remember why you were successful in the first place.* As they say down South, *"remember to dance with who brung you!"*

Ask lots of questions when business is going well. Question all aspects of your business, big or small. Are you recognizing both internal and external threats? Are there new competitors to learn from or be wary of? Are there internal inefficiencies that ultimately may turn into problems? Look for new ways to deploy your marketing dollars. Review your sales data to make sure you're getting the right bang for the buck.

Look for new and creative ways to give great customer service. Communicate with customers and associates as often as possible. Forge bonds with each. Make sure your priorities are in order. Improve aspects of your operation that are within your control. Don't worry: there will always be other things to keep you up at night!

MASTERING BASIC PHONE SKILLS

Great phone skills will start relationships off on the right foot!

The other day I called ahead to order my lunch at the local hot dog stand. As patience isn't one of my virtues, I thought I'd have my lunch waiting. The conversation went something like this:

Hello, I'd like to order a chicken sandwich.

What kind of chicken sandwich?

Grilled, with ketchup and mustard

(No comments from the gallery, that's just the way I roll)

What kind of chicken sandwich, we have 11 on the menu (he was starting to grow exasperated)

I paused for a second. I was trying to remember what sandwich I liked and then this gem came out!

Sir, come on....I'm swamped....what do you want?

With that, I hung up and went to McDonalds (I really have to stay out of that place). I was mortified. Have you ever had an encounter like that over the phone? How did it feel? Did it make you want to spend more money with that company? The sad fact is the person I was speaking with was the owner. I recognized the voice from having been there (too) many times. What kind of example was he setting for his people?

Did he realize that there was a human being on the other end of the line? I wasn't calling to waste anybody's time. I wanted to buy something. That's why customers call us, because they want to patronize our businesses. Most customers don't complain when something like this happens, they simply vote with their feet and head over to the *"golden arches"*, just like I did. They elect to spend their hard earned dollars elsewhere.

Equipping our associates with the proper phone skills is required if we want happy customers and a successful business. Do people jump when the phone rings? If twelve people are working, then twelve people should run when the phone rings. The initial conversation may be the first (and possibly the most important) customer "touch point". Of course, there are many individual touch points that make up the overall experience. Are all important; however, getting off on the right foot can effectively lay the groundwork for the whole encounter.

Here are a few phone tips that will help you keep your customers and cultivate new ones.

- **Smile through the phone** - it's actually good for you.

Studies show that smiling is actually good for your health! Even fake smiling. The very act reduces harmful hormones and elevates the levels of good hormones. Try this to exercise to help you learn to smile while talking on the phone. Buy a mirror and keep it by your desk. The next time you talk to a customer on the phone, study your facial reactions.

Believe it or not, the person on the other end of the line can feel the smile through the tone of your voice. Smiling causes your facial muscles to shift. Your voice will sound different. Re-record your voice mail greetings both on your office phone and your cell phone. Be cheerful. Exude energy. Remember, callers may never have heard your voice before. Hopefully, while leaving a message for you, they will be thinking, "Wow, what a happy person!" Once you have this down, you will be well on your way towards the next key point.

- **Show enthusiasm** – it's much easier to make a good first impression.

In face to face situations, only a small percentage of communication is verbal. The rest is how you look, what kind of gestures you make, and your facial expressions. Over the phone, it's even more difficult because a caller can't see what you're doing. (Sometimes that's a good thing). In our early days as our company evolved, I made it a practice to study the way our associates interacted with customers I coached our associates to be more enthusiastic, so that our customers would never feel like an interruption, or worse, that we didn't value them. Have you ever called a business and genuinely felt welcomed by an enthusiastic greeting? How did it feel? You probably wanted to spend money with that person.

- **The caller is not a nuisance** – don't make them feel like one!

There is only so much your caller needs to know about why you can't come to the phone. If someone isn't available, say something professional to the caller. It's more preferable to say, "She isn't available right now, but she will call you back" than to say "She is busy right now, can she call you back?" When we say we're busy, the tendency is for the caller to feel like a nuisance or an intrusion. Asking customers to call back is a cardinal sin and chances are the caller will never call again. It is not the caller's responsibility to return the call. Often, if you change a few words, you can convey a far different and much more positive message.

- **Have patience** - slow down!

Ask my wife how ironic it is to hear me talk about patience. She claims that when they were handing patience out, I was somewhere else probably getting a Diet Coke. I didn't always realize, in customer service situations, the importance of patience until we switched the way we answered the phones. The new approach was to say "Thank you for choosing... or "Thank you for calling..." instead of simply blurting out our company name.

The result: our associates slowed down and gave our customers a chance get their thoughts together. We stopped rushing our customers. The last thing anybody wants is for customers to feel like an interruption, or too feel that the associates have other (better) things to do.

- **Use positive words** - get rid of the vague and uncertain words.

Use words with positive meanings. Try saying "I will" instead of "I will try." Use "certainly" instead of "maybe." Minor nuances, to be sure, but some words just deliver a higher degree of reliability than the usual murky words. Try to avoid using the word "but." Consider the following sentences.

Sentence 1: We'd like to help you but we can't do that.
Sentence 2: We'd like to help you and this is what we can do.

What would you rather hear? In the first statement, we're saying that we would like to help but.... (The *"but"* negates the part about *wanting to help.*) In the second statement we're saying we want to help and this is what we're going to do. It's much more positive. The best restaurants react with positives rather than negatives. Do you ever call a restaurant on Saturday morning and say, "Can we have an 8 o'clock reservation for 4 people tonight?" Instead of saying no, restaurants that convey positive attitudes will say, "We can seat you at the following times." The end result is the same, you can't have the 8pm reservation; however, the delivery is much softer.

- **Give the caller your name** – it's much more personal.

Even this little tidbit of information makes phone interaction much more personal. It also helps if the customer has to call back for more help. Now, suddenly, they *know* someone in the business!

- **Keep the caller informed** – let them know the next steps.

If you are contacting someone in the warehouse, let the caller know that. It's much preferable to keep the caller informed than to let them *hang* there in silence with no clue to whether you're going to help them or not.

- **Use the hold button judiciously** – call people back instead.

Only put people on hold if you can quickly obtain the information needed to answer their question. Remember that perception is reality. You may only keep a customer on hold for 45 seconds, but to them it feels like several minutes. Unless the information is right at your fingertips, it is much better to return the call.

Is it important to improve your acumen on the phone? It certainly is! Remember, many customers are first introduced to your company with a phone conversation. As getting and keeping customers becomes more difficult, you hate to see little (silly) things turn off customers. Rude and inconsiderate manners can destroy everything you've worked for.

Companies spend massive advertising budgets to get people in the front door only to fall short in critical areas like phone skills. I always wondered if our associates were delivering exceptional customer service on the phone, as they were in the stores. Businesses that deliver exceptional service over the phone have a much better chance of crossing the finish line with their customers.

EFFECTIVE LISTENING

Listening well leads to better management.

The afternoon duo on the local sports radio station is very entertaining. Sometimes a caller will phone in and allege that the hosts said something outrageous about their favorite team. The hosts, having said nothing of the sort, will ask if the caller has been listening to his *imaginary radio* again. If the caller stubbornly continues, the hosts may quickly hang up, but only after shouting, "LISTENING IS A SKILL!"

The comment *"listening is a skill"* is very true. Good listening skills are a valuable tool, one that can help you greatly in business and relationships. How are your listening skills? Be honest! Do you actively listen during conversations, or does your mind wander? Are you thinking of what to say when your turn rolls around? Are you constantly interrupting your conversation partner? Crossing the finish line with your customers and associates requires great listening skills; asking the right questions and listening attentively to the answers. You can learn so much by listening to others. So, who should you be listening to? Start with your associates, the people in the trenches.

Ask your associates how to provide better service. Go to their offices, or to places where they may feel more comfortable. Ask about challenging issues. Ask them to relate something positive that happened recently. Don't dwell on negative situations, but solicit stories and situations where there can be improvement. Probe deeply while making your conversation partner feel comfortable. Listen attentively when they report an upsetting issue. Often, they are more interested in being heard than actually getting you to change a decision. Your associates will be delighted to have these conversations with you. At least once a week, I would walk to a nearby coffee shop with one of our associates. I spent most of the round trip listening. I gained great insight, partially because of the informal nature of our conversations.

Next, talk to your customers. If you want to know what your customers want, ask them. Ask simple questions and listen attentively to the answers. Ask your customers, "What is the one thing we can do to provide better service?" When 9 out of 10 mention the same thing, you know where you can improve your business. Do you ever pick up the phone and call your customers? Everything is email these days. Have a goal to call three customers a day. After one week you will have solicited feedback from 15 people. The results will be more loyalty and many repeat customers.

Be sure to listen to your vendors, suppliers -- and your competitors! Don't believe everything you read or hear, but carefully glean bits of useful information. Find out what is going on in your industry from others' perspectives. Just ask a few good questions and stand back. One thing is certain, people love to talk. Make sure to ask questions that require more than a *yes* or *no* answer. Get people talking! Create lasting bonds. Successful salespeople have great listening skills. They find out more about their prospect (and his or her needs) by listening, rather than talking.

Here are some tips for better listening:

• **Maintain eye contact** - keep your eyes fixed on your partner.

Don't stare (that's creepy); just try not to let your gaze wander. Your conversation partner needs that reinforcement. Does your spouse ever ask "Are you listening to me?" while you're staring at your computer screen. Just ask any football widow (a wife that loses her husband for 16 straight Sundays during the football season), without the proper eye contact, it's hard to know if someone is listening. Keeping the focus on your conversation partner is a great start towards being a better listener.

- **Incorporate gestures** - use facial gestures to show you are listening.

Nod your head when appropriate. Naturally! Not like a puppet, with someone else at the controls. The person talking wants to be heard. Proper gestures reinforce the fact that you are listening.

- **Remove distractions** - put your blackberry in your pocket and leave it there.

Admittedly, I am getting better at this, but it's been a long road. Nothing is so urgent that you must answer your phone every time it rings. I remember once my wife calling me during a meeting. I valiantly tried to explain that I would be able to talk *in a few minutes.* There was a brief pause and then my wife, not to be deterred asked, *"Do you want grilled zucchini for dinner?"*

If it is really important -- like that night's dinner menu -- you will get a call back. If you are expecting important calls, make a different ring tone so you know when the call comes in. Always let your conversation partner know you are expecting an important call. That way, when it happens, it will be less an interruption.

- **Ask clarifying questions** - to understand the situation better.

Ask pertinent questions to help clarify the situation and then carefully listen to the answers. More importantly, show a willingness to listen and understand the situation. This will show a good attitude on your part. Ask open-ended questions that begin with "What?", "Why?", and "How?" Don't lead the witness! Let your conversation partner fill in the details.

- **Do not interrupt** - let other people finish their sentences.

Nothing is more irritating for both customers and associates than having someone else finish *their* sentences. It's intimidating for associates to talk to the boss to discuss difficult concerns. Let them get their complete thought out! The same is true for customers when they are reporting a problem, especially something they consider serious. Let people vent. Let them complete their sentences.

- **Concentrate** – on what they are saying *not* what you are going to say.

A common flaw while conversing with customers is not listening to their complete thought. For example, a customer may be asking a two-part question; however, because you are formulating your answer to the first part, you don't hear the second part. The customer must repeat the question, which is frustrating. It wastes their time and shows a lack of respect.

In many businesses, the company leader thinks he or she has all the answers. Does that describe your business? Do you actively solicit your associates' feedback? Have you ever asked your customers how you can improve your operation? You may not want to know some of the answers, and they certainly won't confide unless you genuinely show the desire to learn from and accept their comments. Start listening to your associates and customers and your business will be stronger for it. Now, if you'll pardon me, I'm going to my imaginary radio. The World Series is on and the Cubs are playing.

HANDLING CUSTOMER COMPLAINTS

Resolving complaints fairly keeps customers.

Do you think your company excels in customer service? Lots of companies do! To be sure, every company probably handles certain parts of the customer service process successfully. Our company was well known for great service, but we knew there was always room for improvement.

One day an upset customer phoned me. That, in itself, wasn't so unusual -- our retail store processed almost 10,000 transactions in a typical week. The atypical part was just how badly we ruined his order. We made not one, not two, but three big errors on his order. Lucky for us, the customer complained.

Most customers don't complain. Why? Many think that companies don't want to hear the complaints, or won't care enough to do anything about them. Sometimes customers are intimidated. Other times, customers believe that nothing can be done. There are other reasons, but the end result is usually the same. The customer decides to shop somewhere else!

The upset customer ordered 12 bottles of wine from our internet site. The first mistake was having only 8 bottles in stock. We didn't have on hand what our site advertised. The second mistake was charging him shipping for a full case of 12 bottles, even though we only shipped 8 bottles. We overcharged him. The third mistake was not returning his phone calls. To this customer, the most upsetting part was making five un-returned phone calls. Clearly, we abused the privilege of having him as a customer.

As long as situations like this were occurring we knew there was great room for improvement. As the expression goes, *if there is one mouse in the house, there are probably 10 more.* When service breaks down, it's very important to quickly handle customer complaints. How you respond can make or break the customer relationship. Respond favorably and you get a whole different level of loyalty. Possibly a customer for life! In many cases, when you resolve a problem satisfactorily, in the customer's eyes, you earn a higher degree of loyalty than that of a normal customer, one who has never had a problem with your company. Respond poorly, and you probably will never see that customer again.

Let's examine how to handle customer complaints.

- **Let the customer explain the situation** – let them vent.

This first step is *crucial.* The fact is that the customer placed their trust and confidence in us and we failed him. Does this sound harsh? Probably, but this is how customers feel when we let them down. Part of the process of repairing the relationship is to let the customer explain the situation. Let customers vent and speak their feelings. Let them use their own words. It's simple in theory, but not easy to actually sit there and listen. It has been my experience in a lifetime of customer interactions that if we don't listen to the venting, no amount of generosity will help the customer forgive us for our error. It just won't help in the long run.

Whether you speak in person or over the phone, make sure to use visual and verbal clues so the customer knows that you're listening. Let the customer speak. Don't interrupt. Resist the urge to jump in and start defending yourself. Don't think about what you're going to say when your turn rolls around. Concentrate and just let the customer get the problem off his or her chest.

- **Respond with empathy** – show that you care.

Apologize, and do it in a timely fashion. According to Jack Mitchell's book (2003), *Hugging Your Customers,* you must do it "quickly," in 2 or 3 days -- not weeks. If you wait too long, the customer will develop a grudge, which will be much harder to diffuse.

The other day we ordered a salad at a local restaurant and I went to pick it up. It was prepared incorrectly. My wife ordered the chopped salad and was given the Cobb salad. I called to ask for a credit and the manager called us back a few minutes later. She responded with great empathy. Obviously, this wasn't a situation of life or death, but she apologized profusely. She stated that she was "horrified" about the error. To be sure, *it wasn't that big a deal,* but the important thing is that she didn't minimize the error. She went the extra mile.

Let me explain. Yes, this was *just* a salad; however, the significance (of the salad) was not for the manager or the restaurant to decide. It was important to my wife, *the customer*, and that's all that mattered. They handled the situation properly.

Show sincere empathy. See the problem from the customer's point-of-view. Show that you understand how the customer feels.

Customers just want to be heard. They want to be appreciated, and for companies to acknowledge that they are spending their hard-earned dollars with them. I talked to a long-time customer the other day about this topic. Doug mentioned that, in his opinion, "A customer problem or complaint is the single best opportunity a business person has to make a lasting, positive impression," When customers complain, we have the opportunity to turn a negative into a huge positive. Unfortunately, most people don't understand that kind of opportunity. Instead they become difficult to deal with and feel threatened.

I believe this goes to the root of complaint resolution. Complaining customers want to be appreciated. We've all been in the following situation. You hold the door for someone and they don't acknowledge you. They don't say "thank you." Does that get under your skin? It gets under my skin. It's all about showing appreciation. That's why responding in a caring, empathetic, and appreciative manner is so important.

After the upset Internet customer had finished venting, I apologized for our error. I didn't make excuses, as excuses only make situations worse. I simply told him I was sorry he had to take time out of his busy day to handle the matter. I did so in a genuine way. I was sincere. Remember, it wasn't for me to decide how important or trivial this matter was to the customer. My job was to care that we had failed to handle the situation correctly, and to fix it.

- **Ask how you can make the situation right** – don't be cheap!

The local restaurant that prepared the wrong salad, for my wife, sent us $50 in gift cards, even though the salad only cost $12. Wow! It was pretty surprising. If they had asked me what they could do to *make the situation right*, I would have just asked for a refund. Often, when you ask that question, the customer will want less than you were willing to give! It is vital in these situations to give something of value, but its okay to let the customer decide what is equitable for them.

To be sure, there were many times when simple, honest errors were made by our organization, and customers expected us to go to the moon to make things right. Those situations weren't easy and, fortunately, those people constituted a small minority of customers. Most people were reasonable. In the case of the incorrectly charged internet customer; he simply wanted to be charged the correct shipping cost. I would have done more to keep him as a customer, especially after he had done us the favor of complaining. He let us know where problems were occurring and we were able to fix them.

Always keep in mind that customers would rather shop somewhere else than complain. Crossing the finish line with our customers requires that we make the little things count. It is critical that we address matters that might seem trivial to us; however, are important to our customers.

Just the other day, I was discussing a prospective business deal with a local company. After a few emails, one morning, the sales person sent a terse missive stating that she would be "unavailable for the rest of the day and all further questions would be answered the following day."

Perhaps she had other things to do but that's not the point. I know I'm not the only fish in the sea; however, there were other ways to convey that message. By the tone of her email, I felt like an intrusion; a thought that probably never crossed her mind. My sense is that she would be surprised to know that *one measly email* ultimately caused me to second guess my decision to give business to her company.

The little things really matter to customers. Always be sure to let the customer vent. Respond with a caring, empathetic attitude, and find out how you can *make things right*. Be fair. Never make the customer feel bad. Never let the customer feel like they are an interruption. Don't let customers get away. Always respect the fact that customers have choices and they have chosen you. Maintain a positive attitude, even in the midst of unpleasant situations. Keep a winning attitude and your customers will never want to cross *your competitors'* finish line!

EXCUSES VS. ACCOUNTABILITY

Turn heads by maintaining your integrity and honor.

Have you seen all the toy recalls in the news lately? Mattel and Fisher-Price are recalling millions of toys due to concerns about elevated levels of lead. As you probably know, numerous studies show that lead, in toys, can be harmful to children. Parents can get refunds on the recalled toys, but unfortunately, they must jump through many hoops to get their money back. They have just a short time to fill out and file complicated forms, while the toy companies can take several months to send coupons. Yes, the parents that return toys have only one option - using the coupons to buy more toys from the same company! They can't get their money back. Only in America!

There has been much finger pointing. Everybody is blaming everybody else. The toy companies are blaming Chinese toy manufacturers by saying that their safety measures aren't sufficient enough. The Chinese manufacturers are blaming their vendors, accusing them of making shoddy or dangerous toys. They're also saying the problem could happen to toys made anywhere, not just in China.

Doesn't anyone take accountability? Doesn't anyone take responsibility? Shouldn't the U.S. toy manufacturers take some of the blame? Mattel, in a major public relations offensive, has apologized, but at the same time has shifted blame elsewhere. In my career, I have received quite an education in how to handle problems and mistakes. One thing I learned: ***Don't make excuses***.

Customers don't care what you went through to get the product on the shelves or into their hands. They don't care how hard it is to find people to effectively answer the phones. They don't care about the challenges of making deliveries in an urban environment. They don't care if the "one of a kind" fancy machine broke down. It's not to say that customers are heartless; they just have so many choices and so many demands on their time. They want what they want, when they want it!

Remember the Tylenol scare in 1982? That year, four people in Chicago died from swallowing cyanide laced Tylenol. Even though Johnson & Johnson had nothing to do with the tampering; (a criminal act was committed by someone not associated with the company), they took full responsibility. Johnson & Johnson didn't make excuses. They put the public's safety first. Their handling of the crisis is legendary and a great example for all to learn from.

Many companies, at one point or another, face a crisis. Even more make mistakes and errors that look bad in the eyes of customers. It's simple but not easy to effectively manage bad situations. It is simple to blame others, but not easy to stand and take responsibility like Johnson & Johnson did in 1982. Crossing the finish line with customers requires that we manage untimely crises and other problems with integrity and honor. That we take responsibility and not shift blame elsewhere. In many cases, it says more about your company when things go wrong, than when they go right. When things go wrong, customers have a different playing field on which to measure your competence, and your integrity, as a company.

Here are a few things to keep in mind.

- **Be up front with your customers** – tell the truth.

In this day and age information can be disseminated very quickly. *That's a good thing and a bad thing.* For example, if you have to notify customers quickly of a problem, you can do so in an efficient manner. On the other hand, if your customers in cyber space want to spread news of your follies for all to see, they can, with just a few keystrokes. As it is, many customers don't trust us! According to the book by Jeannne Bliss (2006), *Chief Customer Officer*, "67% of surveyed consumers don't believe the brands they do business with keep their promises." Ouch!

Back in 1982, Johnson & Johnson immediately distributed warnings to hospitals and distributors and stopped their advertising. They used the media to alert people not to take Tylenol, all the while absorbing a $100 million hit. To be sure, most problems aren't life or death, like this tragedy, but Johnson & Johnson's behavior teaches us all the benefit of honesty and fast reaction to a problem or crisis.

Our customers have many choices. One way to encourage customers to cross *your* finish line is to earn their trust and confidence. Have you ever dealt with a business that you felt was behaving dishonestly? We all have at one time or another. How did that feel? Put yourself in your customer's shoes. Nobody likes constantly looking over their shoulder; hoping that their vendor is being honest with them.

From time to time, our wine stores would deliver wine to customers. Sometimes, orders would be forgotten. We were only human. The key was admitting our mistakes to the customer. Sure, we could always say the truck was on the way (and cover up for our error); however, it was much better to admit our mistake and keep the bond of trust we worked so hard to develop with our customers.

- **Take immediate measures** - quickly correct the problem.

Johnson & Johnson issued a national recall of all Tylenol and dumped an estimated 31 million bottles. They didn't want the public to worry about consuming their product. They worked tirelessly to keep the public informed about the problem. Some people asked why they were doing so much, when they hadn't caused the problem. Their reasoning was simple, and neatly stated in their mission statement. Johnson & Johnson's ultimate responsibility was to their customers, the medical professionals using their products, and the communities where they worked. That is why they reacted like they did. In their view, there was no *other* way to react.

In normal business circumstances like our typical delivery mishap above, immediate action was essential. A sizable portion of our delivery business was for events and parties. Sometimes, guests would be arriving for a party and our truck wasn't there yet. Understandably, the hosts would be anxious and upset. Taking immediate measures and not making excuses was crucial. It was important to fulfill the obligation we had made to the customer. Do things always go as planned? No, of course not and when breakdowns occur, it is important to do whatever is necessary to make the situation right.

- **Restore confidence** – get it right the next time

Late in 1982, Johnson & Johnson re-introduced Tylenol to the market. They turned to customers, listened, and addressed their fears. They worked hard to regain the public's trust. They introduced new tamper-resistant packaging. To entice customers, they offered coupons so that consumers could try the new product at a discount. Their sales people educated the medical community. The goal was for everybody to rest easy and confidently take Tylenol again.

There are other reasons to handle these situations correctly. Numerous studies show that consumers like to tell "customer service horror stories" to as many people as possible. In fact, according to the Small Business Administration, 85% of us will tell 9 people about a bad service experience.

This worried me greatly when we made errors in our business; that customers would be telling stories (about us) to their friends and associates while I was at home sleeping. Great service providers know that the way problems are handled is more important than the problems themselves.

- **Eat a little crow** – give some financial incentive to the customer

It is important to give something of value to the customer when problems occur. In fact, Tylenol was discounted heavily so that consumers would try the product again. When our business made a mistake, we usually *ate* a few dollars. Maybe it was free delivery or a complimentary bottle of wine. The point is that we offered a little token of our appreciation. It didn't have to be anything spectacular. Sometimes, we simply sent a heartfelt thank you note or a handwritten letter of apology. Typically, customers expect something of value so it is best to understand that giving something of value is part of winning back their business.

Companies and individuals foul up every once in a while. After all, we're only human. Luckily, our errors actually help us develop better systems and practices. It helps to see ourselves from a *different chair*, from a different perspective. The critical component is accepting responsibility for our mistakes and immediately working to regain our customers' trust.

In the words of Noel Capon (2001), author *Key Account Management and Planning,* "No matter what business your firm is in, the only thing that matters is securing, retaining, and growing your customer base." Taking accountability inspires customer trust in your honor and integrity, and brings customers back after problems occur. Accepting responsibilities, and not making excuses, helps you survive the middle miles with your customers and moves you closer to the finish line.

HIRING THE WINNERS

A winning workforce will help welcome happy customers.

I remember the summer of 2004 quite clearly. While the country watched the Democratic and Republican political conventions, we were putting the finishing touches on our second retail location in the Chicago suburb of Downers Grove. For our entire history as retailers of fine wine, we had only one store. We moved from time to time, but we always resisted the urge to expand. As the summer was ending, we were almost ready to cut the ribbon on the new store.

Opening a second store after a long history as a one-unit retailer posed quite a few challenges. Choosing the proper location was the first priority, but once that was done the next task was selecting the right team for that store. We had always been a family-run business with one location, so (in that environment) it was relatively easy to spread, maintain, and cultivate our core values and culture.

With the second store, we had to be sure that our customers would see similar faces, personalities and attributes, as they had become accustomed to in our flagship store. Choosing the right staff was critical.

Here are some methods that helped us assemble a great team in the new store. The results were spectacular.

- **Hire friendliness and communication** – over job specific skills.

I remember Denise's interview like it was yesterday. Denise was an excellent candidate, but she knew very little about wine. We took a chance because she was incredibly pleasant and personable. Customers loved her, and so did I because she always had a smile on her face. In past years, we expected our associates to be more knowledgeable than our customers; but *changing times* ushered in different needs. What was different? The Internet came of age!

The Internet gave customers access to information typically reserved for wine professionals. In fact, with all the information available online, our customers often knew just as much as we did. Sam's could very easily have had an associate in Spanish wines who had never been to Spain; yet one of his or her customers might travel there frequently to taste wine and learn about the region. These days, with so much information available to consumers, companies still need knowledgeable associates. However, other qualities are equally, if not more important. Customer needs have shifted. Other important attributes have emerged.

For example, planning a wedding or a party is pretty stressful. The beverages may be pretty far down the totem pole, but 3 weeks before the blessed event, *everything* feels monumental. A service business like ours needed people like Denise to gingerly lead customers through the process in a calm, friendly way. That was the important part. Anybody could have matched the *rubber chicken with the perfect chardonnay,* but it was the intangibles that made the difference. It was much more valuable for our customers to feel they had a *friend in the business.* That's what Denise represented to the people she helped.

- **Creatively interview** – find better ways to vet prospective job candidates.

Implement new ways to interview and select the right candidates. Have more than one person interview each candidate. Develop better questions to understand a person's character and moral compass. Be creative. One time we visited someone's *My Space* page. What a shocker! Right there in black and white were the words, *"love to stay out all night and party!"* For those not familiar with the alcohol beverage business, it's really, really good to stay away from those people.

Administer some skills testing. We always found it useful to know the level of one's wine experience, not only to determine their knowledge level, but also to see if they were truthful in their own assessment. Do some role playing. Ask difficult questions. "What would you do in this situation?" Ask how the applicant handled commitments in their last job to get an idea how they think. To determine flexibility, ask about a situation where the applicant had to be flexible. Notice their tone. Read their body language. Look for visual clues. Try to determine how they *actually* felt about the situation.

- **Resist the temptation to hire anybody** – wait for the right candidate.

As I look back, one of our primary hiring goals was preventing substandard candidates from ever seeing their first day at Sam's. We realized that there were enormous costs associated with making bad hiring decisions. The toll on the company, both financially and emotionally, was unlimited. When we hired people and then, quickly, let them go, our unemployment rate went up. Further, bad hiring decisions caused us to waste money on education and training. Most importantly, we wasted time and energy working with people that weren't a proper fit. For many years we had a habit of holding on to people long after we determined they weren't helping the company. We finally realized that the longer the person stayed, the harder it became to remove them.

I remember hearing the former Chairman at Motorola speak to my graduate school leadership class. I was intrigued by everything he said, but one thing stuck out in particular. He stressed that the higher a position and wage at which you hired someone, the longer it took to get out of a bad hire. One year to train the person, one year for them to perform (and for you to determine their fit with the company) and one year to remove the person, if it was not working out. I remember thinking, *better get those expensive hires right!*

Hiring the right people is simple, but not easy. It's simple to hire *anyone* when you need *someone*; but not easy to wait for the right person to come along. According to Al Siebert (2005), author of the *The Resiliency Advantage,* "One sure sign that you're hiring the right people is that they make themselves far more useful than their job descriptions call for." We saw this occur frequently. The good hires quickly took on more responsibility than we expected. They thrived on the challenge.

Years ago, we didn't have a human resources position at our company. We implemented that position, created better hiring practices and improved at quickly "sizing up" someone's potential for a future with the company. We began to act more swiftly if there wasn't a proper fit.

- **Cut the underperformers** – don't let them wear out their welcome!

The former CEO of General Electric, Jack Welch (2005), in his book *Winning*, stresses the importance of being "candid" with your associates. In his opinion, associates should always know where they stand with the company. We found this out over time. At first, we weren't so forthcoming with our associates.

Once we started being more candid, we were much better positioned for success. People performed better when we were more honest and forthright with them. If we discovered a problem with an associate, the first step was to have a conversation with that person. We told them what areas or tasks they needed to improve. In many cases, their performance improved drastically. In other cases, it did not; however, at least they knew that the inevitable was right around the corner if they continued to fall short of expectations. Our associates had a clearer understanding on what it took to succeed with the company.

We learned that we had to quickly *cut the cord* when someone wasn't working out, both for the morale of the staff, and in fairness to the underperforming associate. Have you ever worked at a company that retained an associate who was more a liability than an asset? Most people have and know how uninspiring it is to come to work every day and work alongside someone who is not pulling their weight. That's why it is so important to act quickly and decisively.

Selecting passionate, enthusiastic people will help you cross the finish line with your customers and associates. For many years Lasalle Bank has sponsored Chicago's annual marathon. One of their advertisements has always hit home with me. The language reads, *"Alone, you run 26.2 miles, but together we make it a marathon"* My interpretation: you can't run a great business without great people, just like marathoners can't run a successful marathon without all the volunteers and supporters that show up on race day. Once you have the right people in place; revenues, profits and a happy workplace will soon follow.

TRAINING FOR VICTORY

A trained associate starts immediately on the path to success.

How is this for the first day of an exciting new job? You arrive early (of course) and the manager points you in the direction of an experienced associate and says, *"Follow him around and do whatever he does!"* For many years, this was actually the way we started people at our company. There was no elaborate training; actually, no informal training either. We never told the new hire what the company stood for. A quick summary of the company benefits wasn't in the cards either. Our new associates learned everything about the company *on the fly*.

My early years in public accounting didn't start that way. I remember spending a week at a downtown Chicago hotel. The days were spent learning the latest FASB's (don't ask) and the nights were spent downtown on Chicago's infamous *Rush Street* (again, don't ask). I'm not sure *how much* we learned, but at least there was formal training.

You don't cross the finish line with your customers until you educate and train your associates properly. Our most important goal at Sam's (and a critical component of our brand promise) was to educate our customers so when they left our store, they knew more about our products than when they arrived.

According to Pamela Danziger's (2004) book *Why People Buy Things They Don't Need*, "Customers are eager to learn about their passions!" That certainly "hit home" in the wine business. Many of our customers already had thousands of bottles of wine in their cellars, yet they clamored for all the new releases because wine was their passion. We needed educated associates to help our customers. In fact, equipping our associates with the right knowledge base was a great point of differentiation between us and our competitors.

Many of our associates came to us already pretty versed about wines and spirits; however, they still needed to learn about the company, our policies and procedures and other aspects of the operation. They also needed a working knowledge about our industry. We also wanted to improve their knowledge in areas of wine they hadn't yet studied. To that end, we developed a more formal training program that helped our associates provide knowledgeable service. Our customers loved it!

The best service providers continually learn and grow. They keep current on trends, products and customers. They know about their company and industry. The wine business, like all businesses, changes constantly. For starters, each year, new vintages arrive in the stores. Our associates had to know which regions were in favor. Further, we expected our associates to keep abreast of new winemaking trends and to be familiar with the new, popular, wine producing regions. In some years, California wines were *all the rage*. In other years, a different region received all the praise. We always had to have our finger on the pulse of the industry; and to quickly become familiar with the regions and wines that the national wine publications were profiling. All this required a steady emphasis on training and development.

Here are a few areas on which to concentrate your training efforts.

- **Products and services** - does everybody know the full product line?

Have you been in the following situation? You're out shopping and run into an associate who doesn't know his company's products very well? One day, my son and I went to the local office supply store to buy a laminator. There were two laminators for sale. One laminator was $40 more than the other laminator. We asked about the differences, to which the associate replied, "They're made by different companies!" Wow! What a revelation. We could see that ourselves. In the end, we went to another store where the associate was able to help us make an educated choice. We decided not to settle for making a choice based in inadequate knowledge!

Make sure that your associates have some training on the full breadth of your products. That's a tall order, especially if you have thousands of different products like we did. Typically, we hired associates based on regions of the wine world. There were experts in French wines, Italian wines, spirits, beers, etc. The best French wine experts could sell Italian wines and could help other associates if they had a customer who needed assistance across more than one region. Many wine professionals could venture over to the other side (spirits, beer, etc.) and sell a bottle of cognac or recommend the perfect glassware. Our associates became more informed and the result was better service.

To give excellent service all the time, and to uphold our reputation as the top player, we needed versatile and talented associates. To be sure, our associates *couldn't possibly* know everything about every bottle of wine. There were so many varietals, wine producing regions and recent innovations in wine making, so it was virtually impossible for everybody to know everything.

The key was working as a team so that all our associates could help their teammates (by filling in the gaps) when the situation warranted. As Will Rogers said, "Everybody is ignorant, just on different subjects!" Our associates weren't expected to have all the answers. It wasn't a game show; they just needed the courage to ask someone for help if they didn't have the answer.

In our view, more important than the innate ability to choose the right wine for a customer's venison recipe was the *sense and courage* to look customers in the eye and say "I need to ask someone for help!" We stressed that it was *okay* not to have the answer, but that it was imperative to never mislead customers. That would be a gross violation of the trust and confidence they placed in us by walking through our doors. Remember to always act in an honest and ethical manner when conveying information to your customers.

- **Policies and procedures** - hopefully there aren't too many!

Are your associates able to handle most customer service situations? Are they versed on your return policy? Do they need a manager for even the most simple of tasks? Excessive policies and procedures are the curse of customer-focused companies.

Just this morning, I arrived at the bagel store without my wallet. Did they send me on my way *sans* a lox sandwich? No! They floated me a loan until tomorrow morning. What if they had said no? Maybe I would have grabbed my wallet and returned, but more than likely, I would've stayed home. The point is that they exceeded my expectations by taking an I.O.U. from me. They didn't hide behind some silly policy that said "Don't give $10 loans to customers!"

Training should also include the company's non-negotiable points of differentiation. These points may cover how the phones are to be answered, how customers are to be greeted or how to handle complaints. Some time must be spent understanding what is vitally important to the company's mission and what makes the company different.

Train your associates and construct your policies so the first person customers see or speak to can help solve their problems. Be cognizant of their time. Educate everyone on how to deal with difficult and irate customers. While you're at it, have a course or seminar on teamwork. Give tips on how to get along with others.

- **The competition** - know a little about the marketplace.

Your associates should know the competitive landscape. They should have a rudimentary understanding of where the company sits in the marketplace. They should know which competitors compete on price and which ones compete on other parameters.

Everyone should know the company's strategy. Do your associates know what the company stands for and where the company is going? What about the company's goals? Jim Dion, a renowned retail consultant, notes that approximately 56% of corporate workers don't know their company's goals. That doesn't cut the mustard. Imagine if Nordstrom's associates weren't aware of their company's excellent service reputation? What if they thought price was most important to their customers and didn't realize the real reasons customers choose Nordstrom? There would be a real disconnect.

Train your associates throughout the year. It should not be a one-time event. People typically retain only a few things from a training session so repetition is essential. To gain competence, which is defined as the possession of a required skill or qualification, associates should be learning on a consistent basis. Make training a hands-on exercise.

Do some role playing. Watch your associates interact with customers and give pointers. Make sure to do it in a positive manner, as discussed in other places in this book.

Don't forget that training is motivating. How do you feel when you learn something? It's new, exciting and refreshing. Use training as a perk to stay ahead of the competition and retain the best associates. Your associates will reward you by delivering great service to your customers.

THE REWARDS OF REWARDING

Reward the achievement of clearly set expectations.

Mornings don't always go smoothly in my house. The older boys, Josh and Danny, are never particularly thrilled about making their beds; a task they liken to going to the dentist. One morning, after noticing that Danny had done a superbly *sloppy job* with his bed, he and I had the following conversation.

Daddy: "Danny, I think we can do a better job with the bed."

Danny: "No I can't. This is the way I always do it."

With that, Danny made a beeline for the computer while I pondered what had just transpired. Maybe Danny thought that since we never say anything, this was the way we expected his bed to be made. Had we not been clear enough in our expectations?

What about in business? Do your associates ever look at you with a puzzled look on their faces? Do you ever feel that you're not getting through to them?

Often, we don't clearly tell our associates what we expect of them. Part of crossing the finish line and wearing a finisher's medal with your customers is motivating your associates to always give great service. Setting expectations is crucial, as is praising and rewarding the achievement of company goals and objectives. Developing a workforce of happy associates puts a thrill into customer service. The results are higher revenues and stronger profits.

There are several ways to develop a happy workforce.

- **Explain yourself clearly** - make sure your associates understand you.

Do your associates clearly understand your expectations? Do you take the time to patiently explain the company's needs? A friend recently told me of an experience he witnessed with a restaurant client. One of the servers needed a lot of improvement; they were ready to let her go. In a last ditch effort, my friend appealed to the managers that they should tell her *exactly* what was expected and to give her one more night to improve. One of the main reasons new hires fail is because we never clearly specify what is expected of them. One way of teaching may seem clear to some, but extremely unclear to others. Turns out, this person was unclear on what she needed to do. She needed to be told in a different way.

We know that people learn in different ways. Some learn visually, some learn by listening and some learn from a combination of both. Years ago, we used to indoctrinate new people by saying, "Follow *Johnny* around and watch everything he does." Some people can thrive with that odd type of *on the job training*, but others need more. They may need a detailed description of exactly what is expected of them.

The server that was close to losing her job; once the restaurant gave her more details (in a manner she was able to learn from), her performance improved dramatically!

- **Set high expectations** - expect great things.

Set accessible, but challenging goals for your associates. Great companies set goals their associates can reach, but not too easily. David Packard, one of the founders of Hewlett-Packard once said, "Managers should set some objectives (for employees), provide some incentive and then let them do their jobs." He set goals for his troops and expected those goals to be reached.

Conversely, if you expect failure, or accept the status quo, then that's exactly what's headed your way. We always challenged our wine associates to be better. French wine specialists were encouraged to learn about Spanish wines. Spirit specialists were asked to become more familiar with glassware and other accessories. When people were more versatile, the whole team was better. Overall, we were able to serve our customers more efficiently because there were more qualified and knowledgeable people on the floor. It worked out well for both customers and associates.

- **Praise often** – support your troops.

Just like runners need positive reinforcement, especially during the middle miles, associates need the same treatment to give great service. The opportunities to *pat* your associates on the back are endless. Have your managers read *The One-Minute Manager* by Kenneth H. Blanchard and Spencer Johnson (1982). Managers should always be trying to "catch their associates *doing something right.*" Upon witnessing positive behaviors; the authors suggest immediate praise and specific feedback.

Writer Martin Broadwell had it right when he said "Praise is the bullet proof vest for front line service personnel!" Lavishly praise your associates, as you would your grandchildren.

Don't wait for big events to honor your associates. Take the opportunity to recognize the small, positive actions you see each day. If you see a cashier establishing good eye contact with a customer say "Great job maintaining eye contact with that customer!" Be specific. Your associates need specific feedback for the praise to be effective. If it's too general it may have the opposite effect wherein your associates don't understand what they did correctly. That can be frustrating.

- **Reward more often** - demonstrate that you value your associates.

Reward not just the major achievements, but also the minor ones - especially after you have delivered some criticism.

Ask your associates how they would like to be rewarded. It doesn't always have to be financial. Sometimes a handwritten letter from the President of the company will become a treasured keepsake. The key is finding out what is important *to them*, not to you! Good performance can be rewarded in a multitude of ways.

According to David Novak (2007), author of *The Education of an Accidental CEO*, recognizing and rewarding helps build a positive environment. Novak, the former CEO of Yum Foods, used to run KFC

(Kentucky Fried Chicken), and other restaurant companies that employed more than 1 million associates.

At KFC, managers would single out top performers by giving them rubber floppy chickens and $100 bills, a great combination of fun (the chicken) and the serious (the money). He took photos of the winners and proudly displayed the pictures in his office. In a recent interview with *Investors Business Daily*, Novak told the newspaper, "People leave a company for two reasons: they don't feel appreciated or they don't like their boss. They rarely leave for money." He credits the company's explosive growth to the effective motivation of the workforce.

Another example is Wegman's, an East coast supermarket chain. One of Wegman's philosophies is to acknowledge performers by creating new employment opportunities. This ingenuity may be one reason why Wegman's repeatedly makes the Fortune Magazine's yearly " *100 Best Companies to Work For* "list. Instead of hiring inexperienced people from outside the company for new positions, they invite their current associates to apply and be considered first.

Many years ago we started making a concerted effort to promote from within. We immediately saw a change in our associate's enjoyment of their jobs. They started applying for positions for which we had no idea they had an interest. One individual who worked in the warehouse had great computer skills. We moved him to the Internet department where he made a great contribution.

In other cases, we learned of associates who had skills that the company could use in creative ways. One associate, who spent his days entering data, was also an accomplished artist. We displayed his art at a wine tasting which livened up the surroundings. He beamed the whole night! It was very motivating and rewarding for all to see.

- **Celebrate achievements** - maintain a light atmosphere.

Honor your associates every chance you can. Birthdays, anniversaries and outside achievements are all great excuses to have some fun. When someone gives notice and moves on to bigger and better things, throw a going away party. Moving on is an achievement. It means someone is stepping closer to their dreams. Your associates will take note. They will notice that the company is celebrating, even though they now have a position to fill. That's good internal PR. Of course, celebrate whenever the Cubbies win. Don't worry about loss of pro-ductivity; that doesn't happen too often!

Have some fun with your associates. Have a big party and give out awards. Recognize achievements in a grand way. The benefit: your as-sociates will be motivated to stay, and to improve. They will want to be a part of next year's celebration.

The important point is having a fun place for your associates to spend what amounts to a third of their day. I always tried to maintain a light mood as I knew the company's psyche would rise and fall with my attitude. Trust me; it was simple, but not easy. It was simple to desire a motivating, rewarding culture, but not always easy to conduct myself in such a way as to convey that attitude consistently. To me, an easy going style was the way to go. Maybe I was a tad goofy; but that was ok with me.

We've heard it a million times. Taking care of the internal custom-ers will help the external customers. It's true! Let your people know what you expect and praise them when they meet or exceed your ex-pectations. You will like the results, and so will your accountants. Me, I have to make my bed. Apparently, I didn't tuck the sheets in properly this morning.

Giving Good Feedback

Effective feedback should be behavior related.

We can learn so much from our children. Ben, my 4-year old son, is learning to dress himself, and each morning my wife lays his clothes out for him. It's amazing what you learn when you stay home in the morning! With great ceremony, she sets each article of clothing on the floor. His shirt goes upside down, and with any luck, it ends up on his body the right way.

This morning it was my job to help Ben. I laid out his clothing as only a father can -- wrong! I put his shirt down backwards, but not upside down. Ben, knowing a novice when he sees one, shocked me by saying, "You have to do it wrong, to do it right." Wow, I thought. How profound! I started to think that something this simple applies to many management situations.

Companies don't employ robots, they employ people. Each day associates do many things right, and, unfortunately, a few things wrong. What should we do when their actions leave something to be desired? Do we chastise them? Do we humiliate them in front of their peers? Or worse, do we ignore their follies and hope for better results next time?

Companies don't cross the finish line with their customers without first mastering the do's and don'ts of proper feedback. Everybody has heard the logic, *treat your associates well and they will treat your customers well!* It's corny, but very true. How we handle difficult situations is crucial. If we want our associates to learn from their mistakes (and provide better service), we have to give feedback the right way.

Further, you have to do it in a way that builds their confidence and teaches them something, rather than in a way that demeans and embarrasses them. The truth is that people will usually *do it wrong before they can do it right*! In the book *The Profitable Retailer,* Doug Fleener (2005) suggests that "The first mistake should always be on the company. Your associates can't be deathly afraid to make mistakes!" Some of our best customer service professionals didn't start out as the stars they eventually became. They fumbled basic situations just like the next guy. The key to shortening their learning curve was to give feedback and guidance the right way so they didn't repeat the same mistakes twice.

Here are some success factors for giving good feedback.

- **Give immediate feedback** - seems easy, doesn't it?

It's not, because people are sensitive. They don't like to hear that they've done something wrong. It's human nature! Calling someone out for a mistake is embarrassing for them. Despite our trepidation, we must do it swiftly, while the incident is still fresh in their minds. Remember that there is *really* no such thing as viewing criticism as constructive. In our associates' minds, criticism is always negative. How we frame the situation is vital. Instead of leveling criticism, make suggestions and show how things should be done. Offer options and coaching. Show examples.

Delaying the delivery of something unpleasant just makes it more difficult for the supervisor to deliver the news. It also makes it harder for the associate to hear. The more time elapses, the worse it gets for both parties. Don't wait until Thanksgiving to say "Remember that situation *last June*, when you handled Mrs. Jones's order wrong?" That's waiting too long and chances are your associate may have repeated the same mistake many times by then. They may have alienated or permanently lost other customers by doing the exact same thing. Give immediate feedback and your associates will view it much more like a learning opportunity.

- **Provide specific feedback** - tell the associate exactly what he or she did wrong.

Tell the associate exactly what went wrong with Mrs. Jones's order. Give a detailed description. Did he or she enter the wrong delivery time in the computer, or match the wrong wine with her famed Veal Osso Buco dish? (I'd suggest a Rhone from the south of France, but that belongs in another book!). The point is that your comments have to be specific or they will have very little meaning.

As parents, we're taught to apply the same lesson with our children. We're urged not to say, "Good job, son," but instead to say, "Good job, son, for putting your dirty clothes away." This way, your child knows exactly what he did right. The same is true in business. Phrases like "Don't do it that way!" mean very little without more information. The comments should be more specific.

- **Effective feedback should be behavior related** - not based on personality.

When giving feedback that is personal, assume that the recipient will immediately become defensive. Always start with something positive before discussing the problem. Make sure to focus on specific actions or behaviors. Never dwell on the personal attributes of the person causing the problem. The workplace has enough challenges. Don't add petty personal jealousies and animosities to the equation.

My management teams evolved in this area after a rough start. We learned that comments like "What's the matter with you?" or "What were you thinking?" were unproductive and potentially destructive. Vague words and accusations were unhelpful and hurtful and didn't help the cause. We learned that it's always a good idea to start with something positive because it softens the news to come. The individual will be predisposed to receive the feedback more easily and, more importantly, your words will have greater impact. Better behaviors will be learned and accepted.

Always end the meeting on a positive note by praising the individual. Wasn't it Shakespeare who said, "All's well that ends well"? As managers, we must diligently give feedback, both positive and negative. That's part of the job! Always remember these simple ideas and your people will learn from their mistakes. Soon, there will be fewer mistakes and performance will improve. Customers will definitely notice.

REINFORCING POSITIVE BEHAVIOR

Appreciation of employees encourages loyalty.

Have you heard the story about the tree falling in the forest? It goes something like this: if a tree falls in the forest and nobody is around to hear it; did it make a sound? When I sold the business that had been my life and livelihood for nearly all my years, I wondered how my associates would react. Would they really care? Did they like working for me? Would I ever know? I was curious to know if they appreciated the job I had done as the company leader. I felt good about the way I conducted myself, but did they agree? I had always tried to run things a certain way -- to create an environment where people would enjoy spending their time.

I got my answer in a way that touched me beyond words. Some even remembered my birthday!

-*"It would be a pleasure to work for you again."*

-*"Happy birthday! I wish you well, and the best."*

-*"I always could tell how much you enjoyed working with me and the staff here."*

-*"You don't know how much you inspired me and made me feel how a good employee should feel. You always said positive things to me when you came to our store. That said a lot about the company,"*

The last quote was my favorite. It was from a customer service associate -- someone who wasn't making a big salary. She simply liked her job and the company; she wanted to feel like part of a team. To cross the finish line with your customers, you must *first* do the same with your associates.

Simply put, before you can put the thrill into customer service, you must pay close attention to the individuals that interact with your customers on a daily basis. Everybody knows this, though. Right? Not really! To be sure, many companies see the big picture; they understand this important equation. Those are the successful businesses.

You've all heard the slogan: happy employees equal happy customers. It seems simple to *want* your associates to be happy, but it isn't easy to create a culture in which your associates actually *feel* that way. It all boils down to listening and loving. Letting your associates' voices be heard.

Here are some easy tips.

- **Don't ignore the help** - find time to *hear* everybody.

The birthday wish was from a cashier. She took the time from her personal email to wish me a happy birthday *after* I had sold the company. Why? Because every time I went to that store, I stopped by to speak with her. I tried to make her feel like the most important person in the world to me at that moment.

Let your associates be heard. Solicit their input. I once enjoyed a presentation from the Disney Company. The speaker told an inspiring story about how the housekeeping staff was encouraged to submit ideas to help improve the room cleaning process. The staff developed the idea of putting a basket of linens outside each door before their cleaning rounds began. The results were smaller carts in the hallways and an easier, quicker way for *both* guests and housekeeping personal to get around.

Disney management could have dismissed the idea because of where it came from. They didn't; consequently, they developed a better way to do something. The Disney speaker related with pride how great the housekeeping staff felt about their creativity. They truly felt like an integral part of the company.

Inspire others. Get people involved in projects *from the start*. Share what you know. Be committed to involving others. Ask people what they would do in a given situation. Support a culture where managers aren't expected to have all the answers.

Our meetings were informal at Sam's, partly because we were always short of space. We would fit as many people into my office as possible to plan an event or promotion. Typically, I would say something very sophisticated to get the ball rolling. Something like, *"What do you guys want to do for our next promotion?"*

I believed it was much more effective for me to moderate *their* discussion than to lead the discussion by constantly interjecting my thoughts. After all, these were the most talented people in the industry. Sometimes, the creative juices flowed, and we planned something spectacular. Other times, we batted ideas around but didn't get very far so we reconvened another day.

The important part was that our associates were invited to share their thoughts in a nurturing environment. They cared what was happening in the company. My role was to simply listen to their ideas.

- **Address people by name** – people love to hear their names!

My company had a few hundred associates, not exactly General Motors, but enough names to cause confusion. I didn't know everybody's name right away, but it was always my goal to meet as many associates as possible. I always remembered what Dale Carnegie said in his famous book *"How to Win Friends and Influence People."* He said, "There is no sweeter sound in the English language, than the sound of one's own name."

Try to get a few names down and build from there. Learn some facts about your associates. For example, if I didn't know their children's names, I tried (at least) to know whether they just had a baby boy or a baby girl. At a minimum, the associate knew I was trying to take an interest in their lives. There aren't many management acts more powerful (and more economical) than taking a personal interest in your associate's lives. Until you try, you'll never know how special (in your associates' eyes) it is to hear you say "Is the baby sleeping though the night?" Try it!

- **Say something positive** - to each associate once in a while.

We had an associate who always went out of her way to please our customers. She was, figuratively, worth a million dollars. I recognized this, and its wonderful effects, and pointed this out by complimenting her many times. She was inspired (see if you can pick out her quote from the beginning of this chapter) and continued this positive behavior.

Compliments are a pretty good value; they don't cost anything. Use them freely but be sure to stick to *safe topics.* Of course, always sincerely compliment desired behaviors, as well as acts of generosity and helpfulness. It's also allowable (and wonderful) to compliment an associate about their children and perhaps something they own like a pretty watch or piece of jewelry, a treasured keepsake they may wear proudly. Be careful when complimenting clothing and appearance. Saying "I like that necktie" is acceptable; however, telling a female associate that you like the way her skirt fits her may be considered inappropriate and deemed to be an unwelcome advance.

Reinforcing positive behavior is one way to say, "Keep up the good work!" A great book on this subject is Jeffrey Fox's *How to be a Great Boss* (2003). Great bosses are constantly "training, teaching, improving and growing their associates." They provide learning experiences every day. They carefully listen and observe. They're always looking for ways to compliment people.

Remember something, especially if you're trying to start being more involved in your associates' lives. *Rome wasn't built in a day.* Take it one day at a time. Try to learn little nuggets about your associates each day. Follow this example from marathon training. When you start training for a big race you increase your mileage slowly. You may run 25 miles for a few weeks and then increase to 30 miles a week before climbing higher. What if you get really busy for 2 weeks and never get your mileage up to 25 miles? Do you jump to 30 miles right away just because that's what your training plan suggests?

No! To do so would shock your system and probably lead to injury. The same is true for new a new effort to appreciate your associates more. Turning over a new leaf is commendable, but don't do it all at once. Take baby steps. If you suddenly begin being everybody's best friend, it will backfire. It will be seen as an insincere act. You will be perceived as disingenuous.

Follow the famous expression, "It's a marathon, not a sprint." Start being more involved; however, do it step by step. Before long, your associates will see a *new you* and you will see great things from them. A happy workforce, one in which your associates enjoy spending their time, will not be far behind.

A Glass Half Empty Or
A Glass Half Full?

Focus on the positive, and profits will follow.

Last December, my family and I took our first-ever trip during the Christmas season. Since I was always in the wine business and working long hours during December, we could never get away. Usually, we enjoyed Chicago's lovely weather in December instead of relaxing by a pool in the hot Florida sun. With excitement, I bought my sunscreen (SPF 1000) and airline tickets for the family and we headed down to the "sunshine state." During the plane ride, I read a great book by Jeffrey Gitomer. Little did I know that the book, *The Little Gold Book of YES! Attitude: How to Find, Build and Keep a YES! Attitude,* would quickly come in handy.

Our family was not accustomed to the throng of warm weather seekers as we had never traveled in December. The line at the car rental counter seemed longer than the Mississippi River. We waited patiently, sort of, for 45 minutes, only to learn that we were at the *wrong place!*

Have you ever made a bone-headed move like that? Done something so silly that it left you scratching your head? Typically, this would have thrown me for a complete loop; however, I was able to draw upon my new, positive mental attitude to save the day! *"Good news and bad news,"* I told my family. *"The bad news: we're at the wrong car rental place! The good news is that we have another funny family story to laugh about for generations to come.*" The children weren't impressed. Neither was the wife, come to think of it!

Situations in life can either be positive or negative, happy or sad. You've all heard the expression, "When life gives you lemons, make lemonade." It's true! Our frame of reference makes all the difference in the world. Had I chosen to be upset by this fiasco, it would have been *my choice*!

Having taken the car rental bus from the airport, we were caught in no-man's-land. I had two choices: take the bus back to the airport, or hoof it a mile to the right place. I hoofed it! (Yes, just a mile; however, I'm not in marathon shape any more. The other day I stepped on our talking scale, and it told me to come back when I was alone!) Unfortunately, that line was just as long. The lady behind me was making all these frustrated noises, muttering under her breath about the long wait. She wasn't happy, but I was relaxed. Inside, I was chuckling because I had chosen not to let the situation get the best of me.

Positive mental attitude is imperative for customer service. If you think your customers are a pain, an intrusion and an interruption, you will treat them like a pain, an intrusion and an interruption. However, if you place them (and your efforts to help them) in a positive light, it can make all the difference in the world.

I recently spoke to the representatives of a call center operation. Their clients were major pharmaceutical companies with fleets of company owned vehicles. I urged my audience to visualize a driver stranded on the side of the road with three appointments yet to make that day. The sooner they got that stranded pharmaceutical salesperson back on the road, the sooner he or she could visit doctors and get important vaccines and medications into the hands (and bloodstreams) of patients. Sometimes, people just need a different way to view situations.

Here are some tips to help you develop and convey a positive mental attitude:

- **Generate enthusiasm**- have a great sense of expectancy each day.

Enthusiastic people have an infectious effect on other people, and because of it, they typically garner more cooperation from others. According to an article in Fortune Magazine (September 21, 2007), Tmobile is rapidly climbing the ranks of wireless providers. One reason is the enthusiasm created by their Director of Customer Service, Sue Nokes. Her associates wait for her visits with great anticipation; they afford her "rock star" status.

One reason for her popularity is that she understands that a fun and enthusiastic workplace pays dividends. Her lifelong belief is that "making the customer happy is a lot easier to do when employees actually like their jobs and feel that what they do matters." She generates enthusiasm and excitement. These feelings are a huge part of maintaining a positive mental attitude.

I started running with my dad when I was twelve. I remember the night before our first run. We went to Hermann's World of Sporting Goods to buy the proper clothing and shoes for our first run. We bought everything we needed, including shorts that by today's standards were *way too short*, and our first pair of real running shoes. We didn't need to buy new T-shirts. We already had drawers that were full of liquor T-shirts with sayings such as "Harvey Wallbanger" (whatever that means). Dad wasn't dwelling on the fact that Mom was forcing him to quit smoking and get in shape. He wanted me, and more importantly, *him*, to be excited and enthusiastic about our new endeavor.

- **See the positive in things** - don't dwell on the negative.

The tendency in life and business is to push positive things to the background and instead to dwell on negative events and occurrences. I remember having a manager who would always complain about orders being filled incorrectly. Of course, I knew that it was important to learn why the problem was occurring; however, I always took time to remind and compliment everybody for all the good things that were happening. I wanted them to remember all the orders that were completed *successfully* and to take pride in all their accomplishments. Be sure to learn from the negatives, but always take note of the positives.

- **Demonstrate positive body language** – check your body language.

Demonstrate your happiness through your body language. Let others see your smile. Smiling shows your warmth, and that you are an open and accepting person. It's actually good for you. The act of smiling lowers harmful endorphins and raises good ones. It shows how you truly feel on the inside. Always greet people sincerely whether on the phone or in person. Try this test: the next time you run into someone that you haven't seen in a while, show, through your actions, that you are genuinely happy to see that person. It will make a huge difference.

• **Welcome friendly criticism** - don't avoid it.

View criticism as an opportunity to learn. Recognize opportunities to see how others view you. If you accept (and don't fear) comments, you may see areas that need improvement. Nobody's perfect! A long time ago, somebody gave me some advice that I will always remember. A friend of mine said "Calm down. Don't be so hyper!" It turns out that my passion and emotion needed to be more reserved when I met someone for the first time. It was great advice.

Learn to ignore people who just want to put you down. Have you ever had a friend or family member who constantly put you down? Did those people lower your self esteem? Learn to spot the people who want to help, while ignoring the others. They're wrestling their own demons. Don't let them affect you.

• **Have a vision** – a blueprint for your success.

Achieving your goals is incumbent on your ability to decide what you want, and then to do everything necessary to get it Most people, although they are not pleased with their current state of life, will do nothing to change the situation. As Herbert Harris (2004) calls it in *The 12 Universal Laws of Success*, they become "satisfied with their dissatisfaction." A success plan is tangible and concrete. Before you achieve success, you must first ask yourself if you are willing to increase your commitment and do whatever it takes to obtain your goals.

In endurance races, like marathons and triathlons, experts talk about "topping off your tank." Eating and resting properly *the night before a big* race, and then adding (topping) off your tank with the proper nutrition the day of the race. Experts say this is critically important if you want to achieve your goals. Don't forget to top off your *mental* tank! Read a few books on positive mental attitude. Learn more about your profession. Keep up to date on current events. Take a class at the local community college. Turn off the TV and grow your mind. Invest in your future. Take the time to change your thought processes. It works!

Remember the car rental mistake from the first paragraph? I could have blamed the travel agent (or anyone but me) and blown off a little steam in the process. Perhaps even saved some face with the family. I didn't, and I felt better for it. I instructed the travel agent to book the wrong car rental agency. It was my fault, but with the right attitude, things turned out okay. Look at the bright side. I ran a mile. At least I worked out!

BECOMING A MORE CARING MANAGER

Associates who feel valued value the business.

Have you ever promoted someone to manager and immediately regretted it? I promoted a young man many years ago and quickly learned it was a big mistake. Boy, did I read this guy the wrong way. Within weeks of his promotion, he had alienated his entire staff by making everybody feel small and insignificant. Presumably, he felt that he would look more important, and more needed, by treating others that way. That experiment didn't last very long as I quickly promoted somebody else to take his place.

What kind of manager are you? Do you want your people to be successful? Are you genuinely happy for your associates when they experience success, or are you always peering around the corner hoping no one is more successful than you? Are you secretly happy when others fail and get egg on their face?

Why is it so difficult to be genuinely happy for the success of others? As children, we cheered for our teammates when they scored the winning run. With our own children we always celebrate their achievements at soccer games, plays, and spelling bees. My children are more likely to be working the sound board or lights at the school production, but rest assured, we always relish their successes. So why is it so difficult to feel happy when others succeed at work?

Short-sighted managers are the curse of any organization. They are constantly looking over their shoulders to see if anybody is gaining on them. Reminds me of my days as an average, somewhat decorated (I'm exaggerating) high school cross-country runner. Common practice for runners was to be continually looking over our shoulders to see who was gaining. Coaches discouraged us from doing this. Instead, we were told to keep looking ahead, and to keep our heads up. This turned out to be great advice for later in life.

The best managers delight in the success of their teams. They realize that their success depends on the achievements of everybody, and that the more the group achieves, the more everyone will grow and develop. It's no coincidence that the companies that perform the best with their customers are always nurturing their associates.

Here are five tips for becoming a better manager:

- **Tell your people** - how much you need them.

Show your people you are happy they are on the team. Let them feel valued. Find out what makes them tick. Make them feel comfortable so they *actually* want to be there.

Managers don't typically excel at this. Authors Adrian Gostick and Chester Elton (2007), in the book *The 24-Carrot Manager*, refute a common reason why managers fail at making their associates feel valued. They pose the following question to managers: Do you tell your spouse you love them? How often? The manager responds *yes, of course!* Typically, the manager's light bulb goes off at this point. They begin to see that their associates can't ever get enough sincere appreciation, just like their spouses!

Unfortunately, most managers prefer the safety of their paperwork and the warmth of their offices. Expressing appreciation and making other feel needed doesn't come naturally. According to a 2006 review by Randstad, the world's fourth-largest staffing organization, 86 percent of surveyed workers said they needed to feel valued by their boss to stay happy. Only 37 percent report having received positive feedback. The great managers always tell their associates how much they need them.

- **Roam the halls and floors** – of your organization.

Get out there and talk to your associates. Compliment your associates in front of other people. That can be extremely motivating. Help your associates with their tasks when you have time. Make it a priority to find ways to make their lives a little easier.

Don't send fancy emails from the corporate office saying you're going to help out at busy times. Just do it! Don't grandstand; your efforts will be far more motivating if others notice your actions, rather than just *hearing* about them.

- **Ask for opinions** - it keeps associates motivated.

You would be very surprised how much your people know. According to Jeffrey Fox, author of many great, common-sense business books, the most powerful words you can say to an associate are, "I don't know, what do you think?" Your associates can really help if you let them. Ask questions. Don't disclose your motives. In many cases, people alter their answers to comply with what they think the questioner wants to hear. Say "What would you do in this situation?" rather than "I think we should do xyz; what do you think?" How would you reply if you were asked like that?

Asking people for feedback makes them want to stay at your establishment, which is sound financial logic. Numerous studies illustrate how expensive it is to replace somebody, anywhere from 2 ½ to 3 times an associate's salary. If your associates are talented (why would you hire them if they weren't?), then they could easily be hired by your competitors. Do the little things to keep them happy.

- **Show others that they are superior** - in at least one way.

Who was the wise guy that said managers have to have all the answers? Leaders and managers don't have to have all the answers. I never had all the answers. I always thought it was much easier to let others shine. Reminds me of former President Harry Truman's famous quote, "It's amazing what you can accomplish if you don't care who gets the credit." Part of delivering exceptional service is motivating associates and making it fun to work with and/for you. Let people feel good. Let them feel they have a great future. Help them be better.

Show your vulnerability. When people feel motivated to help in ways where you might fall short, they are more likely to do a better job. I loved this part of running a company. I used to motivate our associates every chance I could by pointing out things they could do that I couldn't do. For example, our graphic designer had extraordinary talent. He had incredible vision. I complimented him as often as possible. It was so easy to compliment people. It made me feel good and I know our associates felt the same.

- **Create obligations** – for the right reasons.

Some managers create projects, just to make their people look bad. I remember a few cases where managers gave people tasks that they were destined to fail. Those managers' objectives were to look better in *my* eyes. They picked the wrong guy for that nonsense. I wanted everybody to do well.

Work hard to match projects and assignments with your associate's short and long term goals. Do you know your associate's goals? Do you know their expectations regarding their job responsibilities? Communicate regularly with your associates and you will glean this information. You will have more insight into your associates' dreams and aspirations.

- **Show your lighter side** – create laughter.

Life is hard enough without taking everything seriously. Show your lighter side. Have fun once in a while. Laughter actually has many physical benefits. Remember how your mother told you not to worry about everything because you would get an ulcer? Turns out she was right. When we experience stress, our digestive system shuts down a little. When this happens too often, the effects (one of them, ulcers) can be very harmful to our health. Adults laugh on average 17 times a day. Think children laugh more? They certainly do! On average, children laugh 300 times a day. *Improve your laughter statistics.* Have some fun with each other.

Well, that's enough of the medical advice. I'm not a doctor, nor do I play one on TV. Get out there today and compliment someone on your team. Spend some lighter time with your associates. Give them some relevant, timely and specific feedback. Talk with them. Ask for their observations. Implement their ideas.

Observe your associates in action. Reward your associates when you see desired behaviors. Tell them right away while those actions are still fresh in their minds. The results will surprise and motivate you to continue on the path towards becoming a more caring manager. Your team will love it. Remember, you don't cross the finish line with your customers without happy, content associates. Cultivate caring managers and a healthy and happy company will not be far behind.

GRACIOUSNESS IN THE FACE OF ADVERSITY

Every mistake is a great learning opportunity.

Ever heard this one? The waiter comes to the table and the guest says, "There's a fly in my soup!" The waiter replies, "That's nothing, there's a cockroach in your salad!!!!" Don't worry; I'm not booking airfare to appear on the Letterman show. From time to time we all experience bad, odd, or indifferent service in a restaurant. When this happens, how does your server react? Do they respect your feelings? Do they offer to make it right? Do they show respect?

Delivering exceptional service in a restaurant is simple, but not easy. It's simple to *want* to deliver a great experience, but not easy to manage all the moving parts. Just ask that crazy chef on TV that yells at everybody. Further, restaurants are unique because, when you buy something, you get to experience it right then and there. Immediate consumption provides a great opportunity for restaurateurs to either win or lose their customers. If the restaurant provides a great meal and excellent service there will be no complaints.

What about when things go wrong? Handle those situations properly and you will create repeat customers. The result will be a successful restaurant, and lots of happy patrons. Conversely, if complaints are not handled with finesse, nothing good comes from it, including customers who never come back. Worse yet, they can't wait to tell their friends and family!

Here are some tips to use when things don't go according to plan:

- **Respond to problems consistently** – with an eye on your brand message.

The Union Square Cafe in New York City has been providing great service for over 20 years. Their people are hospitable and friendly. When you walk in you immediately know that they are happy you have arrived. One day last month I arrived at their sister restaurant, One Eleven Madison, with my luggage, hoping they would store it until dinner that night. They couldn't have been more accommodating. I tried to help bring my bag to the bell room, but the hostess insisted, saying that it was her job to do so!

It would be inconceivable and inconsistent for them to bark at me if something went wrong in their restaurant, given how nicely they handled my request. It's just not in their DNA to be anything other than gracious. You never know exactly what it takes to cross the finish line with each individual customer. With one simple act, they accomplished that goal with me. I will always return when I am in town.

To maintain a brand, you need consistent behavior. Most companies that fall short with their customer initiatives, fail because their brand promise for serving customers gets forgotten, is ignored, or neglected. If you are genuinely happy that customers are in your establishment, then you should be genuinely happy to help when things go wrong.

- **Apologize, but don't place blame** – no alibis and excuses.

I remember when our son Josh was born. When the grandparents arrived they weren't interested in hearing about the labor or the details about getting to the hospital. They just wanted to see the baby! The same is true in service settings. Our customers don't care if the sous chef showed up late, the oven is broken, or the *salmon* actually swam away. They just want what they ordered in a timely manner. Apologize sincerely, but don't place blame.

- **Spring into action** - make things happen.

When my wife orders a vegetable salad, she asks that all the vegetables be removed and replaced with a completely different set of vegetables. At least she's eating healthy. When she orders a pecan praline blizzard at Dairy Queen, she asks for no pecans. Can you imagine in the fast paced environment of a restaurant, how challenging it must be to handle these types of special orders?

Recently, her restaurant meal was prepared wrong and was taken back to the kitchen. The server immediately sprang into action and brought her a small dish to tide her over for a few minutes. She was thrilled, and the dish was delicious. Not only was the speed of the response impressive, but the little extra dish was completely unexpected, and totally appreciated.

- **Think outside the box** – do something unexpected.

There is a new Westin Hotel near my home that has a couple of fine restaurants. Recently, some associates and I had dinner in their Italian restaurant. We ordered some beverages, but that evening they ran short of something needed to make our drinks properly. The server returned to say he was running over to the Westin's *other* restaurant to get the missing ingredient and he would bring it back for us.

In this case, having the exact beverage was not life threatening; however, the young man showed great initiative. He thought "outside the box" to get us what we wanted. Part of crossing the finish line with your customers is finding ways to delight them. This server found a way to survive the middle miles and to do something special for us. He very easily could have returned to say, "Sorry, but you're out of luck." These things happen, right? On the contrary, a small initiative on his part looked huge in our eyes. We were definitely delighted!

- **Learn from your mistakes** - don't make the same mistake twice.

Once, when I tried to order a dish on the "daily specials" menu, my server said the following, "Sir, that dish is taking longer to prepare than we expected, so we've taken it off the menu for tonight. We don't want to delay your meal." The disappointment was tempered by his, and the restaurants, honesty. This restaurant had made a mistake with one selection, but instead of having a long line of unhappy customers, they elected to stop making the dish that evening. Should they have known of the problem ahead of time? Probably, but at least they were learning from their mistake. Don't make the same mistake twice. Every mistake you make should be a new one.

The restaurant business isn't easy, which is why the rate of failure for new restaurants is so high. There are many moving pieces. Customers arrive with high expectations. In his famous book, *Setting the Table*, Danny Meyer talks about writing the last chapter, and making it a great one. Go the extra mile to solve problems, even those you didn't cause! Show empathy! Have the resolve to learn from your mistakes! The results will be great relationships, strong customer loyalty, and healthy profits.

ACCEPT AND LOVE CHANGE

As the business climate changes, so must the company.

Only a few things stay constant in life. For me, one example would be my hair follicles. Last year I was bald; this year I am *still* bald. The Chicago Cubs haven't been to a World Series for nearly 100 years, and despite teasing us with the playoffs again this year, that will probably never change. Other than that, we live in a state of constant change. Things change around us all the time.

Dell Computers is changing. According to reports in many newspapers and magazines, they will now sell computers in retail stores, a marked departure from their previous philosophy. Dell has always been a mail-order and online company, with no retail presence. All of their computer systems have typically been manufactured to their customers' specifications, and it would normally take a few weeks for the new computer to arrive. Now, there are more ways to acquire their computers and you can bet that Dell will struggle just like most companies do when change occurs.

Even billion-dollar companies change course when their performance starts to suffer. Certainly, at one time of another, the rest of us will encounter circumstances that force us to re-think things. Does change affect all of us? Yes, as the expression goes, *"Change is inevitable; except from a vending machine."* Has your company ever been forced or elected to make major changes? To be sure, companies are always making minor changes, tinkering with this policy or that procedure and creating new ways of doing things.

The experts say that change is good; however, your associates may (probably will) be resistant. Innovation can be difficult and painful. Part of staying in the race and crossing the finish line with customers and associates is avoiding stagnation. Standing pat is simply not an option, and there are ways to handle change in a positive manner. The result is that happy associates will stay longer, and the lower turnover will lead to a better company. Keep a few things in mind and you will spend more time serving customers and less time managing uncertainty.

Here are a few tips for executing change:

• **Eliminate uncertainty** - communicate with your associates.

Do you ever hear people whispering in your place of business? Failing to communicate leads to gossip around the water cooler and a loss of productivity. Your associates desire and want to know what issues and opportunities the company is facing. They deserve that respect. I can't think of many things more important after managing thousands of associates than keeping fear to a minimum. Honesty is the best policy. Explain how the changes will affect them individually. That's what they really want to know.

Reaction to change is predictable, but manageable. It involves managing fear. The leader must try to understand associates' perception of the changes taking place. How severe do they think the change will be? Do they perceive it as good or bad? The leader's job isn't to eliminate the fear, that will never happen, but to reduce it to a manageable, healthier level. Life is uncertain, employment is tenuous, and every employee needs reassurance that they are not at risk

• **Demonstrate a flair for the dramatic** - rally the troops.

How dynamic and persuasive is your company leader? The time of change is the time to shine. I'm not suggesting the pageantry of a Gettysburg address; however, some drama is helpful. Organize sessions where a leader conveys the reasons for the changes. For many years our motto was price, service, and selection. One year, due to longstanding competitive pressures, we decided to raise some prices to achieve higher margins. This was a marked departure from our past operating philosophy.

We convened a store meeting on a Sunday night, complete with Power Point and pizza. We took great pains to help people attend, even chartering a bus from the city to the suburban location where the meeting was taking place. We wanted to make it easy. I took our associates through the history of the company. I explained how the competitive landscape had changed and laid out a carefully crafted set of reasons as to why we needed a shift in direction. My goal was to create focus and urgency. For so many years, we had been the winners in the wine wars. Without starting a panic, I wanted to explain why it was important to keep winning. I tried to connect with the crowd and to show a side of me many of our associates had never seen before.

My management team and I believed that by carefully explaining the reasons for this change we would have a much better chance of getting our point across. To be sure, not everyone was thrilled, but many people liked that the company went to such lengths to convey this message. It was simple, but not easy. Simple for me to stand on a platform and speak about treating the customer like a king, but not easy for all the associates and managers to get on board. We had to explain and motivate. Rallying the troops and explaining our reasons definitely helped convince most that the price increase was warranted. Our associates were reassured and energized.

- **Motivate** – by including all levels of the organization.

Change has a much better chance of success if the decisions are made by more than just the "head honchos." We developed a new brand promise, a short and concise service statement, as part of our plan to raise margins. We also introduced a new customer service initiative we called the "GRAPES." We asked people to be on committees and challenged everyone to help develop the new strategy. We achieved greater acceptance and a greater sense of urgency by showing that we wanted everyone's opinion. As a result, we got off to a great start.

- **Walk the talk** - practice what you preach.

Maximize your chance for success by continuing to talk about the changes after the initial pomp and circumstance has died down. Nothing lets the air out of a balloon faster than a quick return to "business as usual." What do you talk about on a daily basis? Do you ever talk about the direction of the company, or do you spend more time talking about paperwork and other trivial things? Do your associates know your mission statement? Do they know why the company exists? Be prepared to have individual meetings, over a free lunch or dinner if needed, to hammer home your points. Take all questions and objections with a sense of humor and plenty of information. Encourage everybody in a nurturing, honest manner.

Don't forget to communicate with your customers about any changes that affect them. Be prepared. Customers don't like change very much. They are creatures of habit; and loyal to their own comfort. Explain things very carefully.

A local wine store in town just eliminated their frequent shopper program for a new one to be introduced a few months from now. Customers were told they had only so many days to redeem their points, and were given very little explanation about the new program. I know that if we had done that, customers would be up in arms, especially if we had not given them a coherent explanation. We never would have proceeded in that manner.

Remember, customers and associates want to know what to expect from us. That's their right. They're giving us their money and their time. Everybody expects change. In fact, the only constant in this world *is change*, to quote the famous expression, and it occurs at a breakneck pace. Speaking about changing from a century of futility, let's not forget the Cubbies. Next year is right around the corner. Maybe the World Series is a possibility after all!

MOTIVATING AND MAKING IT FUN

Make buying painless and enjoy the repeat business.

Those who know me know that I like my cell phones! It should not come as a shock to learn that I finally broke down and purchased the *iphone*. I resisted as long as I could, and much longer than my family imagined. Unfortunately, in the end, the curiosity got the best of me. I have to say, it was quite a revealing experience. In spite of many news reports detailing long lines and activation hassles, I experienced no such trouble.

My boys and I bought the *iphone* at the local Apple store. Despite moderate Sunday traffic, we managed to get in and out of the store pretty quickly. Apple has set this up to be a relatively painless experience, *except for the price tag*. You buy the phone in the store and activate it by hooking it up to your computer at home. Apple's music software (iTunes) takes care of the rest. I must admit, it was *really* cool and took less than 10 minutes to install. It was intuitive and easy to follow. Fortunately, there were no complications.

More importantly, the cell phone buying experience wasn't like the normal trip to the wireless store. Often, the buying experience is far from fun. On our last visit to the local wireless store to buy a new blackberry, my son and I thought we were on the famous game show, *The Price is Right*. First, the price was $150, then $200, then $250. It kept changing. My son, an 11-year old with a Blackberry, wanted the Pearl and had saved enough money; however, because he recently bought another phone, the carrier wanted to extract the highest price. We left the store far from satisfied.

Crossing the finish line with your customers requires that you first get to the *starting line*! The best companies and organizations know that it is essential to motivate customers and make buying fun. If you get this part of the equation right, your customers will return again and again.

Here are a few tips to help you motivate and make it fun for your customers and associates.

- **Keep things simple** - don't over-complicate!

By creating a simple activation procedure that customers could do in the comfort of their homes, Apple greatly enhanced the retail experience. The painless activation procedure left me wondering why each visit to the wireless store takes so long.

The last thing you want is for your customers to feel negative emotions about your company or brand. Minimize elaborate systems that ultimately turn off your associates and customers. Make sure your return and sales policies are flexible and accommodating. Offer value relative to price paid. Customers abhor receiving poor value. Learn how to tell when your actions frustrate your customers. Judge *what* your customers and associates are saying, not how they say it, so you pick up valuable clues about your business. As Yogi Berra (the famous baseball player) said, "You can observe a lot by just watching!" Start watching and keep things simple.

- **Motivate your associates** - reduce cumbersome policies.

Many times I have watched disinterested associates dutifully enforce ridiculous rules and policies. The most ingenious part of Apple's strategy was the activation process. If problems cropped up, all that nonsense occured in the customer's home. Not in the store! Imagine if the activation took place at the Apple store. Instead of helping eager customers hand over $500 for their new devices, Apple's associates would be helping people sync their address books. Let's see; selling new phones or resolving sync issues like why Aunt Betty's email won't appear. You choose what seems like more fun!

Whenever we considered new policies and procedures, we always first considered what effect it would have on our associates' willingness desire to deliver great service. Do you review your policies regularly? Do you consider how it might feel should the shoe be on the other foot? Once in a while we would come up with something and then, while looking at each other, instantly agree that none of us would be happy complying with this requirement *ourselves*. We went back to the drawing board to craft something better.

It's important that managers create situations where service people can thrive, not the opposite. On a recent trip to the deli, my friend asked how the tuna was prepared. Without batting an eyelash, the server asked if she would like a taste. I was astounded. Usually, my friend explained, you have to ask for a taste, but she had never seen the server come right out and offer one. Maybe I'm not dining in the right places!

- **Keep a light atmosphere** - everything doesn't have to be so serious.

Just walk into an Apple store and you will know what I mean. The stores are bright, the lighting is perfect, and there is music playing throughout. The Apple associates always seem to be enjoying their work. Apple works hard to remove obstacles that might otherwise impede their associate's enjoyment of their jobs. For example, lines at check-out are stressful for both customers and associates. Apple's associates have little hand-held devices that act as cash registers for those paying with credit cards. This kind of ingenuity makes things go more smoothly.

Even shopping malls are getting into the act. Most men would rather have a root canal than go shopping with their wives. I recently read in *The Chicago Tribune* that Woodfield Mall in suburban Chicago plans to open a high definition TV lounge this winter. Shoppers (er... men) will be able to watch the Cubs lose in vivid clarity while their wives shop for shoes, handbags, jewelry and the perfect hat for that perfect dress. Hey, you have to accessorize!

I always tried to maintain a light mood. I tried to make the little things count. Sometimes, we would have balloons for children. Other times we would serve hot dogs in front of the store, for customers and associates. One day we served some lightly salted popcorn that everybody loved. Little touches, like playing music, worked wonders. The idea was to make it fun for everybody to be there, just like the environment at the Apple store. Now, if you will excuse me, I have to load some Barbra Streisand on the new phone!

THE POWER OF DELIGHTING
A CUSTOMER

Thoughtful gestures delight customers and bring goodwill.

It used to be a privilege when I could spend nights in great restaurants, all the while knowing someone else was picking up the check! As the President and owner of a prominent wine business, I was usually the *chosen one* when producers and winemakers came to town. I only accepted a few of these invitations over the years as they involved me staying up way past my bedtime. The winemakers typically brought their newest vintages and suffice to say a good time was usually had by all.

Several things have changed since those days. Most notably, I have less hair than before and I'm no longer in the wine business. Those fancy meals are a fading memory, having been replaced by more pedestrian meals where I usually *foot the bill.* There is one meal, however, that is still very clear in my mind. One evening, a famous Barolo wine producer was in town, and several of us ventured out for a semi-casual steak dinner. At that dinner, I witnessed something spectacular that helped me understand why it is so important to care about customers.

At the next table there were eight businessmen in town for their national convention and they were having a grand time. They happened to order the Barolo wine produced by my dinner companion. I'll never forget his expression! His eyes grew wide and his smile grew wider when he realized what was happening. He had come a long way and right before his eyes, consumers were buying his wine! No spectacular wine review could rise above that for excitement! He immediately approached the table to introduce himself, and engaged in several minutes of conversation with the businessmen. It wasn't until later that we learned that he paid for the bottle, and the one after that. He never mentioned it to anyone, probably not wanting to draw attention to his act of generosity.

Wow! What an incredible gesture! I was stunned, as were all the people at both tables. Had he simply introduced himself, we would probably have thought that was pretty cool. But he went the extra mile, and that was priceless. Part of crossing the finish line with your customers and creating happy customers, is finding ways to delight them.

Customers have choices today like never before. There are many more stores, restaurants, producers and manufacturers than just a few years ago. The internet has raised the ante even higher. More choices! Do you run a not-for-profit? Those causes pop up every day. To be sure, these organizations help good causes but, without some pizzazz, they will eventually get lost in the crowd. No business or organization automatically rises above in the new economy where choices are abundant. The most successful businesses and organizations find ways to stand out!

Does your company do anything to stand out? Are you creating emotional experiences for your customers? Many experts talk about the customer experience. Scott McKain (2005) in his book, *What Customers Really Want,* suggests that "…What many organizations are terming as *customer service* is, in fact, *customer processing!"* Do you serve customers and clients, or do you simply process their requests? Do you ever wonder why customers patronize your business? If you can't put in words why customers should do business with you, then your customers may have the same trouble. Always ask the tough questions.

Finding a way to separate your company from the pack is essential. Organizations and individuals that find a way to differentiate by delighting their customers move ahead of the competition. They are rewarded with positive customer attitudes and great word-of-mouth advertising. Their customers cross the finish line, which brings loyal customers, repeat and referral business, and the resulting profits.

Here are a few simple ways to delight customers.

- **Go the extra mile** - and involve your associates.

At our stores, we asked, and expected, our front line people to retrieve the shopping carts from customers just so they could say "Thank you!" or "Have a nice day!" We understood the importance of the customer's last impression of us. In fact, most studies show that what happens *last* will be what your customers remember more than anything else.

Of course, nothing is more important than a consistently well executed service encounter; however, typically, what happens last is what stands out with customers and clients. Sometimes, I stop by my accountant's office. My accountant, Ted, not only walks me to the elevator, but also accompanies me down to the first floor. Does this seem insignificant? I thought so at first until I realized that we spent the entire ride down talking about family and other non-business topics. Ted was doing his part to build a relationship with me. He was *going the extra mile*!

At Sam's, I helped retrieve shopping carts right alongside our associates. I did so for two reasons: first, it got me out of my office to interact with associates and customers (which I loved doing), and second, it allowed me show our associates what I expected. Showing appreciation in *my own way* was very important to me.

There is no right or wrong way to show appreciation. As a marathon runner, I walked in races all the time; yet, when I finished races, I usually had a pretty respectable time. The trick was to run fast while I was running, so the "walking breaks" didn't slow me down that much. The point is that there is more than one way to run a marathon as there is more than one way to show appreciation. The important thing is to *show it!* You can appreciate people all day long, but if you don't show anybody, they will never know.

- **Don't promise the world** - under promise and over deliver.

Keep it real, so when you do more than expected, the results are magnified, a much better alternative than the opposite -- doing less! Our store had a reputation for being able to make deliveries anywhere in Chicago that same day. On some days, we joked that our customers *thought we had helicopters.* We never promised more than we could deliver. Even if we knew someone's order was going out on the next truck, we still promised delivery for later that day. That way, when the truck arrived much earlier than expected, the customer was thrilled. Conversely, if the truck had mechanical problems, the customer was none-the-wiser, as we probably still accommodated their request. Managing expectations was crucial for our business, as it is for all businesses.

- **Do the unexpected** – and surprise someone.

It's rare these days for an associate to walk a customer to the item they are looking for, and more common for them to point. Do your associates act like statues? Are they afraid to stray too far from their comfort zones? Do they view walking with a customer halfway around your building as a chance to bond, or do they see it as an interruption or inconvenience?

One way to delight your customers in a retail setting is to leave your station to help a customer find something. As Peggy Morrow (2006) explains in her article, *Eight Keys to Creating* a *Customer Service Culture,* "Never point to an item. Always walk someone to an item and engage them in conversation." It can be frustrating and difficult to navigate around a large store. I used to see people all the time come in Sam's (a wine store as big as a football field) with their mouths wide open. Some even tried to turn around and walk out, before we interceded and helped them to feel more comfortable.

- **Take ownership** – of problems.

Do your associates take ownership of problems or do they shift responsibility (or blame) to somebody else? Don't play *hot potato* with your customers. Are your associates more apt to say, "He is gone for the day" or will they say, "He is gone for the day, but I will help you in his absence?" The proliferation of choices for consumers has gone hand-in-hand with the increased demands on their time. The last thing customers want, need, or deserve is to be passed from one disinterested associate to another. Teach your associates to take charge of customer situations, to rise above pettiness, and to ignore whose issue it was originally. Stress teamwork! Explain that if everybody shares the responsibility, at the end of the day it all evens out.

Remember the wine producer's incredible gesture? The morning after the producer bought the wine for the table, the whole industry was buzzing about his insightful action. Word circulated like crazy! Many people called me to see if it was true. With such a simple, inexpensive gesture, he created buzz and good will that money could not buy. His customers became fans for life that day.

Appreciate Your Customers
And Show It

Few things are as important as saying "Thank you!"

We've all been in the following situation. You're carrying a brief-case or bag, yet you gamely hold the door for somebody in the middle of a driving rainstorm and that person fails to appreciate your efforts. No smile, no gesture, no acknowledgement of any kind. How does that feel? Be honest! It aggravates me to no end. Usually, I will say something like "No, no -- you go ahead -- I'll take care of it!" *At least I feel better*! I crave appreciation just as much as the next guy.

Is it important to appreciate our customers and each other? You bet it is! According to William James (a 19th century pioneering Ameri-can psychologist and philosopher), appreciation is the most basic, and most important, of all human emotions. People desperately crave ap-preciation. Why? James believed that we inherently want to feel good, to feel wanted, and to feel needed. The beautiful thing about showing appreciation is that it doesn't take long at all. It is one situation where brevity is in order. Showing appreciation will definitely create better results and help keep loyal customers.

- **Say "Thank you."** – make sure to utter those magic words.

We bought a house and the builder never said "Thank you." A beautiful new, shiny home for which we met with the builder on many occasions, and he never said thank you. Not when we made the down payment. Not when we were picking which shade of black counter-tops would match our dishes the best, (who knew there could be so many different shades of black!) and not when we closed and moved in. Not one single time.

It begs the question, did he appreciate our business? I guess we'll never know. Imagine, on the other hand, if he had sent a small gift card to the Home Depot! Even the most minimal amount of concrete appreciation would have created quite an impression on us. We would have told everyone, and by so doing, created great word-of-mouth advertising for the builder.

Is word-of-mouth advertising beneficial for businesses? Yes, but only if a positive message is being conveyed. Stand out from the crowd, but for the right reasons. Andy Sternovitz (2006), author of *Word of Mouth Marketing – How Smart Companies Get People Talking,* defines word-of-mouth marketing as "Giving people a reason to talk about you, and making it easier for that conversation to take place."

There were several things the builder could've done to get us talking about his company. What about the easy act of sending a housewarming card? Stopping by to say 'hello' would have been a nice touch. Any small token or gesture to show his appreciation would have been appreciated by us - and productive for him.

- **Send a quick note** – take that extra step in appreciating your customers.

Send out thank you notes! I used to do that all the time. It was simple, but not easy. Simple to talk about thanking customers, but not easy to write the notes on a Monday morning when I had a ton of other work to do. My goal was to write thank you notes for every transaction over $500. On some weekends that could mean a nasty case of writer's cramp! Following through was essential.

Thank you notes should have a bit of personalization and should be mailed in a timely fashion. Our cards were computer generated, but I personally printed the customer's first name and signed each card my-self. I personalized many cards with a simple comment. For example, if a customer was from Indiana, I would simply say "Thanks for making Sam's a part of your trip to Chicago." Nothing earth shattering, but it was a bit more personal, nonetheless. The many years in business taught me that customers are not fools. They can sense insincerity a mile away.

- **Send out small gifts** – it's the thought that counts!

The lack of appreciation I encountered in the home buying process gave me an idea. I approached a local automobile dealership with the idea of sending gifts to people who recently purchased cars. The gift, one bottle of wine in a gift box, was generous enough to get the point across. Imagine, you've just spent anywhere from $35,000 to $100,000 on a new car, and you get a small gift in the mail. Talk about going the extra mile and doing the unexpected! The dealer had great success with the program; the feedback he received was incredible, all for a inexpensive $33 per unit, including taxes and shipping! They were thinking outside the (wine) box!

The great news is that the effect of such generosity goes far beyond the cost of the gift. According to Reinartz and Kumar (Harvard Business Review, *"The Mismanagement of Customer Loyalty"* HBR '02), "An unexpected surprise generates exceptional word-of-mouth advertising." As a result of their thoughtful deed, the automobile dealership started to benefit from the residual effect, in the name of positive vibes in the community. They paid a small price.

- **Late is better than never** – do it after the fact if you have to!

Years ago, I was reviewing some sales records and one customer's name appeared at the top of every report. No matter how I sorted the report or what variables I searched for, his name appeared. He was our best customer! Suddenly, I felt a bit uneasy, a bit queasy. You know that feeling. When you suddenly realize you've been missing the boat on something. Have you ever felt that way? I was ashamed that I had never spoken to this customer.

Don't get me wrong. He was *far* better off working with our talented wine specialists; however, I still wanted to reach out and thank him for all his business. Nervously, I dialed him. I told him I was ashamed to make this call and that I had been remiss to never properly thank him for all his business. He interrupted me, not to hang up on me or tell me off, but to tell me what an extraordinary business I had and how wonderful our associates had always treated him. My fear of making the call turned to elation. He was *thanking me* now. He actually thanked me for taking time out of my busy day to call him! What a pleasant surprise! I had called to express my appreciation, and in turn, received a great feeling back.

- **Make up reasons** – to say "thank you"

Actively look for other ways or situations to say those magic words. The American Management Association suggests a few other times when a thank you is appropriate. To be sure, this may seem like common sense; however, often times the basics get swept under the rug because of our frantic lives.

Appreciate your customers when they compliment your company. Don't just shrug it off. Say "Thank you!" Appreciate your customers when they suggest you to their friends, when they offer comments or suggestions, and when they help you serve them better. Don't forget the times where they have exercised patience with you and the situations when they tolerated your mistakes.

As previously mentioned, crossing the finish line with your customers is simple, but not easy. It's simple to say that customers are number #1, or that customers are our top priority, but it is not easy to treat them that way. Sincere appreciation goes a long way!

By the way, the house turned out great. The countertops superbly matched our dinner ware, just as my wife had planned, that is, until she bought new dishes!

CHEERING FOR OTHERS

Winners in the business world are flexible and likeable.

The 2007 Chicago marathon was run on a really hot day. Temperatures were 70 degrees at the start, and in the mid to high 80's, with humidity, by mid-day. I never ran a marathon under such extreme conditions, although I came close. I ran in 1979 (as a naive 13 year old) when the mercury topped off at 84 degrees. I remember the challenges those conditions presented.

Many marathoners were probably eating their pasta Saturday night and worrying plenty about the race conditions. They were probably making decisions on how to run the following morning. What would you do in that situation? Would you back off your original racing plans or run as fast as you expected to run before they announced the weather? Would you observe the conditions and adjust your plans accordingly? I know what I would do, and suffice to say, it's probably good I wasn't running!

Those runners with flexible personalities probably changed their plans and aimed simply to survive the elements. Hopefully, most runners adjusted their plans, drank plenty of fluids and re-figured their pace charts. Some probably skipped the race altogether. Not a bad idea! The inflexible runners, those who stayed with plans they made prior to learning about the extreme conditions, likely had a pretty tough day!

Is being flexible important in business? You bet it is! There is no script in business -- or life for that matter. Most things don't go according to plan. Customers throw curve balls; so do venders and associates. We know Mother Nature spiced things up for the marathoners. With few exceptions, the absolutely rigid don't fare so well when times call for adapting to challenging circumstances.

Are there other success criteria in business and life? Yes, there are many personality traits that will enable you cross the finish line with your customers and associates.

Here are a few to keep in mind.

- **Be flexible** – go with the flow.

Be adaptable. Welcome change as an opportunity, not a threat. Keep a positive mental attitude. Learn how to frame decisions properly. Gather intelligence. Learn from your experiences. Celebrate your successes and find fun in your failures. Admit your mistakes and learn from them.

As I contemplate the flexibility required for last Sunday's race, I am reminded of the race I ran in 1989 under similar conditions. It was nowhere near as warm, but was still a warm day for October. As an over-confident 23-year old, I ignored the experts when they cautioned to modify pace when the conditions weren't quite right. I went out way to fast. By 6 miles, I was feeling the heat. It would be a very short day due to my inability to be flexible and to adapt to the circumstances.

- **Be likeable** – assemble an attractive personality.

Tim Sanders (2006) in the book, *The Likeability Factor* talks about how your personality can "Be your greatest asset or your greatest liability." Have tolerance for people. Always control your temper. Give people the benefit of a doubt. Display tactfulness and think before you speak. Be friendly and supportive. When people like the source, they are more likely to trust the message.

We spend our lives trying to get people to pick us (starting with gym class!) and continuing on until we find ourselves wanting our customers to pick us. Being likeable, either personally or as a company, is tantamount to success. Customers loved coming to Sam's. It was a likeable experience and they told us on many occasions.

Display initiative. Everybody loves "go getters" except those that are more comfortable sitting on the couch. Help out. Help your teammates. Don't leave others in a lurch. I remember a particular New Year's Eve many years ago. New Year's Eve in the wine and spirit business is a *battle* right up until the store closes. I asked a young guy to stay and help. He declined, saying he was "going home to watch the NFL playoffs!" I was stunned. He made a poor decision. Follow Stephen Covey's advice (1994) from his timeless book *First Things First.* "Avoid politicking, backbiting, blaming, accusing and confessing each other's sins." Instead, be proactive, sincere, sensitive and aware. Be a giver, not a taker.

Generate enthusiasm. Have a great sense of excitement for every day. Be optimistic. Don't take people for granted. Everybody wants to be recognized and acknowledged for their efforts. Treat everybody with respect. Avoid rude or uncaring actions. Never humiliate in public or private. Don't accuse or insinuate. You never know who might be your boss some day!

- **Be real** – so people know what to expect from you.

The most effective leaders and customer service professionals are perceived as real from the inside out. They conduct themselves in a consistent manner by always spot checking their attitudes for the right behaviors. A favorite example is the following: You meet a friendly executive at a networking meeting. The conversation flows as if you've known the person your whole life, so you schedule a follow-up meeting at a local restaurant, all the while wondering where this person has been all your life.

This is where the inconsistency starts. The friendly individual you met the first time now rears a very different head. He barks orders at the restaurant server and complains about everything under the sun. The manager comes over and he berates him in front of everybody. This is inconsistent behavior and a red flag. Genuinely real people have the same attitude all the time. They don't deviate from the norm.

Always be transparent. Be honest and ethical in everything you do. Keep your promises. Show great character. Be credible. Unfortunately, most people don't believe what they hear, so credibility is crucial. Be self assured, but check your arrogance at the door.

- **Be a good communicator** – show humility.

Don't brag. Be modest. Don't talk about yourself and your accomplishments, unless people ask. If others take an interest in what you've achieved, instead talk about what you like about what you're doing. Tell how your work helps others. I remember many business situations where humility was helpful. Longtime customers would come in our store on a busy Saturday in December gushing about how great business seemed. After politely saying *thank you,* I always turned the conversation around to them. I asked them about their businesses, their lives. Customers enjoyed that; it made us both feel great.

- **Be interested in others** – and not so enamored with yourself.

Bring out the best in others; it will help you too. It costs nothing, but can mean so much in the long run by building your reputation. In the book *How to Win Friends and Influence People,* Dale Carnegie (1937) says that "You can win more friends in 2 months by taking an interest in others than you can in 2 years by trying to get people interested in you!" Nothing could be truer. Give value to others before you ask for something in return. Build rapport, build friendship. As Jeffrey Gitomer says, "Be excited about the prospect of helping others. Help your customers solve their problems."

Mentor the new guy in the office. Give your associates permission to speak freely. Recognize their lives outside of work. Solicit your associate's ideas. Engage them in decision-making. Respect confidentiality. Invest time in others. Relish in their successes and respond to their feelings. Compliment others as often as possible.

The great news is that, according to numerous studies, being likeable is actually good for your health. *The Likeability Factor* talks about this phenomenon. "When we're likeable, we feel our likeability reciprocated, and that in turn increases our self esteem." People with higher self-esteem have less stress, which, as we know, causes many serious ailments.

Thankfully, many of my friends running this year's marathon were able to *survive the middle miles* and cross the finish line! To be sure, it was probably an arduous task for all the runners.

What about you? Whether your foot hits the pavement in a race, or in business, or in personal relationships, the traits mentioned in this chapter (and this book) will help you succeed. Remember to be yourself. Be honest and likeable. Take a genuine interest in other people, just like millions of spectators cheer for others on race day.

THE FINISH

The Final Straightaway!

Only 385 yards to go! Thanks for reading *Surviving the Middle Miles!* I hope you will find the preceding 26 tips useful for improving the relationships you have with your customers and associates. I promised 26.2 ways, and we have to finish the .2, so here goes.

The majority of great service is treating people, customers and each other, the right way. It's simple, but not easy! It is simple to want to differentiate ourselves and our businesses from our competitors, but not easy to have the right systems, attitudes and behaviors to get the job done consistently.

As you recall (from this book's introduction), the 1989 Chicago marathon was my first attempt to qualify for the Boston marathon. That year, after inviting my friends and family to the finish line, I failed to appear, succumbing at the 14-mile mark.

The next year I tried again. This time I told fewer people and made fewer predictions, but the result was the same. I dropped out at 14 miles. Why couldn't Phidippides, the founder of the marathon distance, have died after 14 miles, I thought to myself!

Not to be deterred, the next year I tried again. This time I didn't tell anybody. Well, I told my wife, so she could have the *car waiting at 14 miles!* Unfortunately, the result was the same. By the time I reached that *annoying* 14 mile mark, I was taking my number off and, once again, making plans for next year. Just like my cursed Cubbies!

Next year came several years later. I took some time off.

Why did I have so much trouble with the marathon? Why were the middle miles so difficult for me? I'm not exactly sure, but I do know that few people achieve their goals on the first try. Often, it takes many tries before we cross the finish line in whatever we're trying to accomplish.

You know the expression, "There is no free lunch!" These words remind us that most anything worth having or achieving doesn't come easy. Customer relationships are no different. Effective human interaction is the key. Terms like appreciating, respecting, nurturing, delighting, motivating, listening and loving are more than just words. They are concepts that help you survive the middle miles and cross the finish line, in business and life.

In 1997, I re-entered the world of running. My thirties were upon me; beer and fast food were *upon me*. It was time! I told myself I could survive the middle miles. I trained all summer. I was ready.

As I approached the 14 mile mark, the light bulb went on in my head. Ever been there? Do you know what the moment feels like when you *finally* figure something out and it all seems so clear? That's what happened! Instead of worrying about how I would feel at the 23-mile mark, I did the little things to get to 15 miles. What a novel concept: making it that far in the marathon!

I remember those miles very clearly. I looked up instead of looking at my shoes. I enjoyed the scenery. I paced myself and drank plenty of fluids. I slapped hands with children lining the course. I trudged on and made it to 18 miles, then 20 miles. Finally, in a journey that seemed to start 10 years earlier, I crossed the finish line!

I ran 10 more marathons including Boston. To be sure, those other 10 race days weren't *walks in the park*; however, I did have a sense of what it took to cross the finish line. I survived the middle miles -- and you can too!

You have to remember that it is simple, but not easy. It's what you do every day, every mile that counts. It's the little things like simple, random acts of kindness. Perseverance is the key! Developing your plan for showing your customers you value them, and then on race day, when they've chosen you, having the dedication, desire and determination to see it through.

Before you know it, you will have crossed the finish line, in whatever race you're running!

ACKNOWLEDGMENTS

There are many people who have helped me bring this book to you. There isn't enough space to mention them all, but I do want to give thanks from the bottom of my heart to:

Jill Rosen, my wife. Your support (and editing) is much appreciated, not to mention all the time you've allowed me to *hang out* with my laptop. Thanks for being my best friend.

Josh, Danny and Ben Rosen, my children. Thank you, boys, for laughing *at and with* Daddy. (In that order, I'm certain.) You have all helped me stay grounded and not to take myself too seriously.

I love all you guys!

Fred Rosen, my dad. In the final analysis, you taught me a ton. Most importantly, you taught me that even though we owned a successful business, we were really no better than anybody else. Ladonna Carlton, my dad's wife. Thanks for being so supportive of my speaking and writing.

Brenda Rosen, my mom. Let's not forget her. Sadly, she isn't around to read this. Mom, even though we only had 19 years together, you taught me to be a good person. As a teacher, you must have taught me a thing or two about writing. Thanks!

Dana Pinsel, my twin sister. Thanks for putting up with me. To be sure, it couldn't have been easy!

All my friends and associates (both past and present) at Sam's Wines & Spirits and in the wine and spirit industry. My experiences are all your doing. You all taught me so much and I couldn't have done (any of it) without you.

Rod Engel, Mark Rubin and Rob Winner, my closest buddies. Thanks for the support. Thanks for being there for me always, but certainly the last couple of years.

Jim Dion, Stefania Pinton and Mike Schall, my friends and part time advisors! Thanks for helping me get started on this new journey!

Denise Casalino and Carole Buchwald, my running buddies. Without you ladies to train with, no way I would've ever crossed the finish line of *any* marathon.

Charlie Bernatowitz, my cover designer. You designed a beautiful cover and captured exactly what I was thinking. I'm not surprised!

And last but certainly not least!

Dr. Barbara von Diether, my editor. Who knew you could find such a beautiful person over the Internet. You had such confidence in my writing. *You let me be me*, with better grammar!

About the Author

Everyone talks customer service, but Darryl Rosen has lived it. He served as President and owner of Sam's Wines & Spirits, a family business started by his grandfather in the 1940's. Under his leadership and unwavering commitment to superior customer service, Sam's grew from a small single operation to a multi-unit retailer with nearly $70 million in sales. Sam's reputation earned Darryl and his team an unrivaled national and international reputation.

Darryl has taken his decades of experience running a successful business and his history of competing in marathons and triathlons and currently delivers presentations and seminars for companies and organizations seeking to "cross the finish line" and grow their businesses. Before joining Sam's, Darryl received a Bachelor's Degree in Accounting from Indiana University and became a certified CPA. He earned his MBA in Marketing and Organizational Behavior from Northwestern University, Kellogg Graduate School of Management in 1997.

Along with his passion for unparalleled customer service, Darryl spends time with his wife (Jill) and three boys (Josh, Danny and Ben), and is always hoping that this year will be the year for the Cubbies! If you would like more information on Darryl Rosen's speeches, seminars and consulting services, please use the following contact information.

www.darrylrosen.com

www.survivingthemiddlemiles.com

Printed in the United States
94505LV00002B/190-1998/A